D1319593

The Author

A Book That Took Sixty Years In The Making

Bloodletting In Appalachia

The Story of West Virginia's Four Major Mine Wars
and Other Thrilling Incidents
of Its Coal Fields

By Howard B. Lee

Former Attorney General
of West Virginia
(1925-1933)

WEST VIRGINIA UNIVERSITY
MORGANTOWN
1969

International Standard Book Number 0-87012-041-7
Library of Congress Control Number 72-94391
Printed in the United States of America
Copyright © 1969 by McClain Printing Company
Parsons, West Virginia
All Rights Reserved
2013

First Printing 1969
Second Printing 1970
Third Printing 1972
Fourth Printing 1975
Fifth Printing 1977
Sixth Printing 1980
Seventh Printing 1983
Eighth Printing 1987
Ninth Printing 1989
Tenth Printing 1990
Eleventh Printing 1993
Twelfth Printing 1997
Thirteenth Printing 2002
Fourteenth Printing 2008
Fifteenth Printing 2013

McClain Printing Company
Parsons, West Virginia
www.mcclainprinting.com
2013

THE BOOK'S TITLE

The title of this book was suggested by a speech made by Old Mother Jones from the front steps of the old State Capitol in the spring of 1912, during the Cabin Creek and Paint Creek strike, in which she said:

> "But I warn this little Governor (Governor William E. Glasscock) that unless he rids Paint Creek and Cabin Creek of these goddamned Baldwin-Felts mine-guard thugs, there is going to be one hell of a lot of bloodletting in these hills."

See page 27.

The Author

ABOUT THE AUTHOR

Howard B. Lee, son of Stephen S. and Virginia Quick Lee, was born in Wirt County, West Virginia, October 27, 1879, in the now extinct lumber town of Shirtzville on Spring Creek, two miles from its confluence with the Little Kanawha River. He was educated in the common schools and summer normal schools of that day. Also, he graduated from Marshall College (now Marshall University), Huntington, West Virginia, in 1905; taught school a couple of years; was a member of the West Virginia Legislature from Putnam County; took his law at Washington and Lee University, Lexington, Virginia; began his law practice in Bluefield, West Virginia, in June, 1909; served four years (1912-1916) as Referee in Bankruptcy; eight years (1916-1924) as Prosecuting Attorney of Mercer County; eight years (1925-1933) as West Virginia's Attorney General; and practiced law in Charleston from 1933 until he retired February 1, 1943. Since his retirement he has lived much of the time in Stuart, Florida. His wife, Ida Hamilton Lee, died in April, 1959. She was a niece of Dr. L. J. Corbly, who was president of Marshall College for twenty years.

Other books by Mr. Lee: *The Story of the Constitution, The Criminal Trial in the Virginias*, and *The Burning Springs and Other Tales of the Little Kanawha*.

FOREWORD

"APPALACHIA" is a term used to denote the vast mountainous region within and adjacent to the Appalachian Mountain System. It embraces both the Blue Ridge and Allegheny ranges, and extends in a southwesterly direction from northern New York into northern Alabama.

West Virginia lies at the geographical center of this mountain area, and for many years it has been the Nation's largest coal-producing State. At the peak of production the industry employed in excess of 125,000 miners. These workers and their families made up a population of 750,000 people who huddled in the grimy mining camps, and lived in company owned houses, which were little better than cow stables in many camps. These deplorable living conditions, starvation wages, illegal, oppressive, and often dishonest practices of many of the early coal operators frequently brought on bloody uprisings that bordered on civil war; and on four occasions required the presence of United States regular army troops to restore order in the troubled mountains.

As incredible as it may now seem, this is a factual book, in six parts. Part One is prologue. Parts Two, Three, Four, and Five tell the true stories of West Virginia's four irrational and bloody "Mine Wars." Part Six describes incidents that took place after the miners were unionized under government fiat in 1933.

Usually, with a factual book, the reader wants to know what the author's opportunities were for acquiring the information upon which his book is based.

In answer to such inquiries, I offer the following:

My source materials were varied and voluminous. In June, 1909, I began my law practice in Bluefield—then the metropolis of a large coal-producing region. Immediately, I became active in politics, and for three successive biennial campaigns I stumped the old Fifth Congressional (coal field) District with and for the Republican candidates for Congress.

During those campaign tours I visited hundreds of mining

camps, was entertained by scores of coal operators and mine superintendents, and met thousands of miners. Also, in time professional business frequently took me into most of the coal counties of the District. Over the years I learned much about the coal industry, the locale of the mines, and the conditions under which miners lived and worked. I also observed certain objectionable practices of the coal operators, and sensed the bitter resentment such practices engendered in the minds of the workers.

In truth, it may be said that this book was sixty years in the making. From 1909 to 1969, I kept a diary of my personal experiences and observations in the State's coal fields. During those years I also kept a scrapbook of West Virginia newspaper articles that told of the important happenings in the coal industry, particularly in the strike-torn areas. They were of great assistance in the preparation of this book. I also received much helpful information from numerous visits to the strike zones. Those West Virginia newspapers are on file in the State's Department of Archives and History in Charleston.

During the first three of those mine wars I was simply an observer. But, as the State's Attorney General, I was an actual participant in the fourth and longest strike and helped to bring it to an end.

But my main source materials were the testimony taken by, and official reports of, the five special committees, State and Federal, that from time to time investigated the prolonged and destructive strikes that plagued West Virginia's coal areas. This evidence and committee reports also are on file in the State's Department of Archives and History.

What caused these senseless outbreaks?

In 1921, United States Senator Kenyon, of Iowa, who headed a Senate Committee that investigated strikes and mining conditions in West Virginia, answered that question in two words:

"HUMAN GREED."

I have never been either a coal operator or a miner, nor did I ever professionally represent a coal company or the miners' union. I have no bias or prejudice in favor of or against either group. My sole purpose here is to state the facts and let the chips fall where they may.

The photographs used as illustrations in the book were taken from forty to sixty years ago and are now faded from age. But they will give the reader an idea of conditions at the time they were made.

In APPENDIX I are the confirming statements of Judge Robert D. Bailey, Honorable Vincent Legg, former Lieutenant of State Police Frank Gibson, and Honorable Sam T. Mallison, who attest to the accuracy of certain incidents related in the book of which they had specific knowledge.

In APPENDIX II are recorded a few isolated acts of union terrorism.

APPENDIX III describes the two most notorious, corrupt, and lawless mushroom towns of the coal fields—Keystone in McDowell County and Thurmond in Fayette County. Both towns are still struggling feebly to stay alive.

The first draft of this book was written in 1936, but it was shunted aside by the press of more important matters. In the spring of 1966 I began a revision of the script, and by the latter part of 1968 it was made ready for publication. In all respects the book is a true history of West Virginia's four major mine wars, and other incidents in the State's coal fields, during the dark and bloody days of the State's coal industry.

Howard B. Lee

Charleston, West Virginia
Stuart, Florida
January 1, 1969

CONTENTS

PART ONE

INTRODUCTION

Chapter   *Page*
1. Prologue 3

PART TWO

CABIN CREEK AND PAINT CREEK

2. The Land That God Forgot 17
3. Old Mother Jones Appears 26
4. Martial Law 32
5. The Bull Moose Special 38
6. Rape of the Constitution 41

PART THREE

THE VALLEY OF THE TUG

7. Bloody Mingo 51
8. The Mock Trials 59
9. McDowell County's Retribution 65
10. War on the Tug 73
11. The Yellow-Dog Contract 78

PART FOUR

THE "KINGDOM OF LOGAN"

12. A "Czar" Rules the Mountains 87
13. The "Armed March" 94
14. Treason 104
15. The Greenbrier Fiasco 112

16. The Passing of the Czar 116
17. Slot Machines and Murder 122
18. The Trial 128
19. End of Logan's Mine Guards 134

PART FIVE
REVOLT IN THE NORTH

20. Operators Repudiate Their Union
     Contract 143
21. One-Sided Injunctions 147
22. Sabotage 151
23. Arrests and Confessions 157

PART SIX
THE DAWN OF A NEW ERA

24. Bloodless Strikes 165
25. Despair and Hunger Stalk the Hills 172
26. Sundown in the Hills 177
27. Epilogue 181

APPENDIXES

Appendix I. Explanatory Notes and
     Verifying Statements 187
Appendix II. Isolated Incidents of Union
     Terrorism 194
Appendix III. Keystone and Thurmond...........203

Index 213

ILLUSTRATIONS

Author .... Frontispiece

PART ONE

Old and new mining camps 5

PART TWO

A group of armed mine guards
   on Paint Creek 21
Mine guards on Cabin Creek 23
Old Mother Jones on Cabin Creek 26
Baldwin-Felts mine guards killed
   and wounded in strike zone 28
Arms and ammunition seized by the Militia 32
Militia encampment on Paint Creek 34

PART THREE

Scene of "Matewan Massacre" 54
Mine guards killed at Matewan 56
Union relief day at Matewan and a
   flying squad of Mingo militia 58
Foreman of jury, and defendants acquitted
   in first mock trial 61
Thomas L. Felts, head of the Baldwin-Felts
   Detective Agency 66

Sid Hatfield, Ed Chambers, and Welch

Courthouse where they died 69

Fruits of a "still hunt" in strike district 75

Strikers' tent colonies in the strike district 76

PART FOUR

Don Chafin and a group of his mine guards 88

Union leaders during the armed march 95

Bill Blizzard at the time of his trial

and Courthouse in Charles Town 109

PART FIVE

Strikers' forts at Grant Town 149
Barrack town of strikers in northern field 152

APPENDIX II

Burning headhouse at Cliftonville 195

APPENDIX III

The famous (or infamous) Dunglen Hotel
at Thurmond 209

Part One

INTRODUCTION

Before entering upon a discussion of the labor wars that disturbed the peace of the mountain coal fields and took so many lives, it is well to look somewhat into the background of those conflicts, and, if possible, ascertain what caused them. I believe that the following Prologue correctly and fairly states those causes.

Chapter 1

PROLOGUE

Most of West Virginia's mountainous coal areas possess great scenic beauty. They are regions where lofty, forest-clad mountain ranges parallel each other like waves at sea, and distant peaks rear their heads among the clouds. In summer, from the highest of these peaks, one looks out upon a circle of mountains on which the rays of the setting sun show gradations of light and color. And in the fall frost paints the foliage into frescoes of livid red, purple, orange, pink, brown, and gold, which blend with the dark evergreens into a panorama of unsurpassed loveliness.

From this grandeur, however, one descends into deep, narrow valleys, dotted here and there with squalid coal camps, and where the rushing streams frequently become foaming torrents. In these narrow canyons the stony wilderness tries to make up to man for its harsh uselessness by its offering of fabulous riches. The territory is a black Golconda where nature is rich, but man, the heir of nature, is poor. Here the coal companies plunder the treasures of earth; and here, too, in these teeming valleys, under the shadows of the shaggy mountain peaks, live and work the State's coal miners.

The trunk railroads follow the main rivers, sending feeder lines up the small branches, along which are located a majority of the mines. Near the mouth of these smaller streams the camps have ample level land. As one advances up these creeks, however, the mountains squeeze closer together, while the valleys become deep troughs. At frequent intervals the canyons contract to narrow defiles as if to safeguard the buried treasures within. In other places the mountains have retreated from the streams and left small patches of bottom land, and these spots determined the location of the mines. The gaunt skeletal tipples (loading machinery), railroad sidings, stores, and other company buildings are located on these small bottoms. Any surplus level land is occupied by the houses of company officials, and usually these have sanitary conveniences. Occasionally, too, there is room for a few miners' houses.

These turbulent streams, once crystallike as they leaped from mountain clefts and wooded slopes, are now black and repulsive from coal dust, and polluted and clogged with mine debris, garbage, animal waste, and camp sewage. In some camps, in dry seasons, the people stand around, study the sky, and hope for rain to wash away the malodorous filth lodged in the creeks. Following a heavy downpour is the only time these open camp sewers are ever clean.

A few of the early pioneers discovered outcroppings of this combustible mineral (coal) at a number of places in the mountains, but they made little use of it. In fact, it was not until the late 1880's and early 1890's that a massive exploitation of coal was begun, and railroads constructed to carry it to market centers. And with this new and powerful fuel, American industry made mighty leaps forward, and the demand for coal grew apace.

At that time the mountain regions were sparsely settled and workers were few in numbers. Also many natives thought that it brought "bad luck" to work underground, and many refused employment in the mines. Miners had to be imported, and there were only two sources of supply: the cotton-growing states of the South, and the over-crowded slums of central and southern Europe.

Between the years 1890 and the beginning of World War I in 1914 the coal operators tapped those sources to the extent of thousands of workers annually. They sent their agents[1] into the South with alluring offers of "free transportation, steady work at good wages, and company houses in which to live."

These agents traveled in pairs, were well armed, and carried sufficient cash to finance their assignments. They were accompanied by a couple of colored "recruiters," who were

---

[1] A number of these agents operated out of Bluefield. I knew a few of them. Usually, they were the toughest of the Baldwin-Felts mine guards.

Top—A typical mining camp of fifty years ago.
Bottom—A modern mining town of today.

skillfully selected for their persuasive eloquence and conscienceless disregard of the truth.

Once at their destination the agents went into seclusion, and the recruiters went to work among the colored population. Mass meetings were held in their churches where the spellbinders described the opportunities offered in this new Eldorado. Those who volunteered were told when the labor train would leave, and also instructed to bring enough food for at least six meals.

The train was in the complete control of the agents, and the coach doors were kept locked until it arrived at its destination. This was for the protection of the passengers, many of whom were having their first train ride. An agent once told me that he believed it was the prospect of a train ride, rather than the promise of steady work at high wages, that induced many of his passengers to leave their southern homes.

The importation of Europe's peasants, however, presented a more complex problem. Expert writers and translators were employed to prepare elaborate brochures in the language of the several countries to be visited by the labor agents. These pamphlets pictured in glowing terms the economic advantages of working in the coal mines of the New World, offered free transportation to the place of employment, and held out the hope of future American citizenship. At that time there were practically no restrictions on immigration, and thousands came by steerage[2] to New York, were hurried aboard labor trains, and rushed to West Virginia's coal fields.

When married, both the European and Negro volunteers were encouraged to bring their families as it was thought that married men made more dependable workers. Upon arrival at the camps, both groups were housed next to the few native white miners in cheap frame shanties that in many instances were unfit for use as cow barns.[3]

---

[2] Steerage passengers brought their own food and paid a fare of one dollar for the entire crossing.

[3] In 1946, Secretary of the Interior, as Coal Mines Administrator, requested the Bureau of Medicine and Surgery of the U. S. Navy to make a study of "housing and sanitary conditions" in the coal mining areas. In its report, dated April, 1947, the Bureau said:

"Ninety-five percent of the houses are built of wood, finished outside with weather board, usually nailed direct to the frame with no sheathing. Roofs are of composition paper. Wood sheathing forms the inside finish. The houses usually rest on posts with no cellars .... The state of disrepair at times runs beyond the power of verbal description or even of photographic illustration since neither words nor pictures can portray the atmosphere of abandon dejection or reproduce the smells. Old, unpainted board and batten houses, batten gone or going and boards fast following, roofs broken, porches staggering, steps sagging, a riot of rubbish, and a medley of odors.

"There is the ever present back-yard privy, with its foul stench-the most common sewage disposal plant in the coal fields. Many of these ill-smelling backhouses, perched beside roads, along alleys, and over streams, leave their human waste exposed, permeate the air with nauseating odors, and spread disease and death.

"...then there is the camp dirt—a mixture of coal dust, dust from the dirt roads, smoke from the burning 'bone pile,' which blend into a kind of grime that saturates the atmosphere, penetrates houses and even clothing, and sticks tenaciously to human bodies."

In both Europe and our South all able-bodied volunteers were accepted. At no time, in either place, was any effort made to screen out the criminal element.[4] Moreover, some of the county and municipal authorities in the South opened their jail doors to all who would join the labor hegira to West Virginia.

One agent told me of a tragic incident that occurred on his return from Alabama. A large Negro was brought from jail by local officers and put on his train. But as soon as the train was out of that county the Negro demanded that it be stopped so he could get off. The agents refused, and in the altercation that followed the Negro was shot and killed. "But I did not know in what county or state the shooting occurred," said the agent, "and besides, I did not intend to let a dead Alabama nigger interfere with the progress of my train. So, I covered the body with some rags and brought it on into West Virginia, where it was buried in a company graveyard, and I heard nothing more about the incident."

Many of the European and Negro criminals worked in the mines just long enough to get a few dollars and then embarked on their own varied criminal ventures. Their diversified operations ran the gamut of crime from petty theft to murder for profit. They became dope peddlers, white slavers, procurers, panderers, operators of gambling joints, proprietors of houses of prostitution; and after the country went dry, hundreds became moonshiners, rum runners, and bootleggers.

The coal counties were overrun with this criminal froth. Jails were constantly full, and circuit court dockets crowded with criminal cases. To meet this situation, the Legislature created special courts in a number of coal counties with authority to try criminal cases only.

Long before the coming of the railroads, the pioneer landowners, ignorant of the vast wealth hidden within their mountains, sold their holdings for mere pittances-from ten

---

[4] The only instructions the operators gave their agents were to "pick workers with strong backs and weak minds, as they give the least trouble."

cents to a dollar an acre. The purchasers, millionaires from the East, through reports of their engineer scouts, knew of these riches, and fattened themselves upon the ignorance of the mountain people. As a rule, however, these land-holding corporations did no mining, but leased their lands to coal operators, individuals and corporations, on a ten-cents-a-ton royalty basis.

Those early individual operators were a hard-bitten breed. Most of them, especially in southern West Virginia, had been coal miners in their native England, Scotland, and Wales. Others had worked in the anthracite mines in Pennsylvania. Being experienced miners, they readily secured operating leases in these new fields. Many of them began business with little more capital than a pick and shovel, a mine car, a mule, a strong back, and a grim determination. By grinding toil—ten to fifteen hours a day—many achieved affluence; and a few laid the groundwork for the fortunes that were later enjoyed by their descendants.[5]

Those early operators were on their own—with no adequate mining laws either to restrain or guide them. They treated their workers and operated their mines just as they had been treated and had seen mines operated in their native lands and in Pennsylvania. They knew no other way.

Through the years, the miners maintained that many operators robbed them of a large portion of their earnings by exorbitant rents charged for the company-owned shanties in which they had to live, by excessive prices exacted for electricity and coal for domestic purposes, and by the unconscionably high prices demanded for goods in company stores, where miners were compelled to trade as a condition of employment.

[5] When I went to Bluefield in June, 1909, there were a number of those old European and Pennsylvania operators still in the southern coal fields. A number, too, had passed on, and the management of their properties had been taken over by their sons, like the late Congressman Edward Cooper, and the late James Elwood Jones, sons of English immigrants. For a further reference to Jones, see Chapter 11. Edward Cooper was in Congress 1914-1918. I stumped the District with him in his two campaigns.

To better maintain their feudal proprietorship, the operators became active in politics, and for half a century, prior to the unionization of the miners in 1933, they were a dominant force in all political affairs—county and State.

Under non-union conditions, the operators could say, and many did say, to their workers: "You vote for the candidates we have selected, or get off the job." In many camps, free primary elections were unknown and a mockery was made of the secret ballot law. The operators selected the candidates they thought were most favorably disposed toward their interests and required their miners to vote for them. Under the caption "I WANT TO VOTE FOR THE FOLLOWING CANDIDATES," they printed the names of all approved candidates on slips of paper called "THE SLATE" and, on election mornings, company-paid deputy sheriffs handed a copy of THE SLATE to each voter as he approached the polls. The voter in turn passed the list to the election officials, also company employees, who marked his ballot accordingly.

This one incident illustrates the political influence of that early coal oligarchy. The State's Workmen's Compensation Law was enacted in 1913. The first commissioner was a former coal operator, who held the post for 14 years. In 1927, Governor Howard M. Gore went outside the coal industry and appointed an insurance man to head the department for a term of six years.

Actuaries employed by the new commissioner reported that the compensation fund was insolvent, and that one large coal company was $300,000 behind in the payment of its assessments. To restore the fund's solvency, the new commissioner increased the assessments against all coal companies, and also brought suit against the delinquent company to collect its unpaid dues. He soon became persona non grata with the coal operators.

Following the general election in November, 1928, the coal operators were in control of the Governor's office and both branches of the Legislature. And in January, 1929, they had a law enacted which abolished, and at the same time recreated the office of compensation commissioner, and authorized the Governor to appoint a new commissioner for a term of six years.[6]

The new Governor promptly named the old coal operator and former commissioner to the "newly created" post. But, on the advice of counsel, the insurance man maintained that his term did not expire for four years, that the new law was unconstitutional, denied the authority of the Governor to remove him, and refused to vacate the department offices. Deeply incensed by such acts of *lese majeste*, the Governor ordered the State Police to eject the usurper and to install the old coal man in his place.

Two stalwart State Policemen forced the office door, picked up the commissioner's chair, with him in it, carried him into the hall and dumped him on the floor, returned the chair to the office and seated the former commissioner in it. They then escorted the ex-commissioner to the street and told him not to return.[7] The State's Supreme Court upheld the constitutionality of the new law, and approved the action of the Governor in removing the ousted commissioner from the department offices.

The "new" commissioner, at first, declared that the defendant coal company, in the suit instituted by his predecessor, did not owe the compensation fund any unpaid dues and directed the writer, as Attorney General, to dismiss the suit. A short time later, however, with the approval of the Governor, he accepted $12,000 from the coal company in full settlement of the claim.

Locally, however, the operators centered their attention upon the election of county sheriffs and assessors. The former had the authority to appoint deputy sheriffs, and the latter fixed the value of their properties for taxation purposes. Controlling sheriffs insured the presence in their camps

[6] The sponsor of this legislation was the late Luther E. Woods, Senator from McDowell County and Chairman of the Committee on Mines and Mining. His autobiography in the *Legislative Handbook for 1929* stated that he was at that time president of three coal companies, president of one operators' association, and a member of the executive committee of another.

[7] *The Charleston Daily Mail* headlined this incident as "High Comedy in the Statehouse."

of a sufficient number of deputies to suppress any union activities, while naming assessors enabled them to keep the tax valuations of their coal properties at a minimum.

In those early days there were no State Police, and county sheriffs were unable to police all the mining camps. To meet this situation each coal company had one of its employees appointed a deputy sheriff to serve as a conservator of the peace in its camp. From that modest beginning, the iniquitous mine guard and company-paid deputy sheriff system came into being; and, eventually, it grew to such gigantic proportions as to become the chief law enforcement agency in the coal counties, even supplanting the duly elected peace officers.

In southern West Virginia these pseudo-officers, called "Baldwin Thugs" by the miners, were employees (called "operatives") of the Baldwin-Felts Detective Agency, an antiunion, labor-baiting, strikebreaking organization headed by William G. Baldwin and Thomas L. Felts with headquarters in Bluefield.[8] Their ostensible purpose, said the operators, was to preserve law and order in the coal camps. In reality, however, they were fearless mountain gunmen, many with criminal records, whose chief duties were to keep the miners intimidated, to beat up, arrest, jail, and even kill if necessary, any worker or visitor suspected of union activities around the camps.

Other operatives were spies, whose identities were unknown, even to the mine officials. They worked as regular employees in and around the mines, mingled with the miners, listened to their conversations, and reported to the agency the names of any workers who spoke favorably of the union, or criticized the management. The agency notified the mine owners, and the suspect was discharged as a "trouble-maker." Sometimes his name was put on a "Blacklist" and passed on to other companies, and soon the victim was unable to secure employment in the industry. Thus the law of the jungle was enforced in the mountain coal fields.

[8] See Appendix I, Note 7.

To keep the miners' union out of the fields, and thus maintain their feudal proprietorship, the operators employed six principal methods of defense and attack: (a) injunctions; (b) martial law; (c) suzerainty over county government; (d) elaborate espionage and spy systems; (e) coercion and intimidation of workers by the use of mine guards; and (f) blacklisting all miners who favored the union.

Injunctions, martial law, and espionage violated no existing laws, but were greatly subversive of the public welfare. But the use of company-paid deputy sheriffs (mine guards) were in violation of law, and frequently resulted in such wholesale killings as to be unbelievable in a supposedly civilized and law-abiding State.

The coal operators defended their spy and mine guard systems by declaring that their miners did not want to join the union, and that such agents were necessary to protect them from assaults by union agitators. This was not true, however, as was clearly shown in 1933 when the miners were unionized under government protection and they joined their union 100 percent at every mine.

Always, the miners asserted that they sought only to maintain their legal right to join their trade union; to regain their lost constitutional guaranties of free speech and peaceable assembly; to abolish the inhuman practices of espionage and blacklisting; to outlaw "cribbing"; to force the installation of scales to weigh the coal mined by them, as provided by law; to enforce their statutory rights to employ their own checkweighmen; to trade where they chose; to compel greater safety precautions; to dispense with all company-paid mine guards; and to enforce the "check-off," whereby the operators deduct union dues from workers' wages and pay them directly to the union.

To attain these objectives the miners had but one weapon— the STRIKE. To make it effective they had to exclude other workers from the pits, peaceably if possible, forcibly if necessary. As always in industrial disputes, other workers were ready to take the places of the strikers, and the operators endeavored to protect them, while the strikers, encouraged by their union leaders, waged violent warfare against both the operators and their strikebreaking employees.

The strikers acted upon the theory that it was their moral right to go to any extreme, even murder, to prevent coal from being mined in strike-bound mines by non-union workers; and their leaders spared no effort to encourage that belief. No matter how unjustified and heartless were the crimes committed by union fanatics, no leader of the union, local or national, ever uttered a word of censure or condemnation. On the contrary, they attempted to justify every crime, supplied able counsel for defendants and tried to block every effort of society to punish the criminals.

Another thing that greatly irked the miners was that the coal operators joined their regional unions, which they called "associations," and also maintained a giant central union named West Virginia Coal Association, with headquarters in Charleston, and still fought to the bitter end to prevent their workers from joining the miners' union.

With the passing years the struggles became more bitter. Again and again the peace of the mountains was disturbed by strikes and violence that bordered on civil war, and required martial law and the presence of both State and regular army troops to restore order.

In the order of their occurrence, the four major and bloodiest of those uprisings are discussed in the following chapters of this volume.

At the time of these industrial disorders, there were scores, probably running into the hundreds, of independent coal operators in West Virginia. They were an individualistic breed—each determined to run his own business in his own way. Time and death, however, removed these "lone wolves" and their holdings were merged with giant companies. Today, coal production in southern West Virginia is dominated by the Consolidation Coal Company, Island Creek Coal Company, and Winding Gulf Coals, Inc. In the State's northern sector, coal production is largely controlled by the Consolidation Coal Company alone.

Apparently, strikes and labor wars in the coal regions are

now permanently ended. A few years ago, the union and the operators signed a "Peace Treaty." The union agreed to forego all strikes in the future. The operators and the union would each designate one representative to negotiate all future wage contracts, and both sides would accept the results.

Part Two

CABIN CREEK AND PAINT CREEK

These two small streams flow into the Kanawha River about ten and fourteen miles east of Charleston, the State's Capital City, and extend southward through the mountains for twenty-five miles. The valleys are narrow gorges between high mountains, and are just wide enough in places for the railroad tracks and the highways that pass up the creeks. At one time those mountains were underlaid with vast deposits of high quality coal—now exhausted. Along these two mountain streams, in 1912-13, was fought the first major Mine War in the history of the troubled State.

Chapter 2

THE LAND THAT GOD FORGOT

In April, 1912, the mines along Paint Creek and Cabin Creek spewed out their 7,500 coal-begrimed miners in the first major strike, and the worst labor war, in the history of West Virginia's coal industry. The late Fred Stanton, Charleston banker of that day, stated that the "Overall economic loss due to the strike exceeded $100,000,000." And the late Bill Blizzard, one of the strike leaders, said that "At least fifty men died violent deaths in those desolate gorges, while the death toll among women and children from malnutrition was appalling."

Nearly six decades have passed since that strike ended. Memory of its tragic days has faded. Only a few individuals are now living who even remember it, and still fewer who actively participated in any of its bloody scenes.

Finally, conditions in the strike zone became so intolerable that a committee of the United States Senate, headed by Senator William E. Borah, of Idaho, came to the area to investigate the situation. In testifying before that committee, Adjutant General Charles D. Elliott, commander of the State's military forces on the two creeks, said: "God is everywhere, on land and sea, but He has not visited Paint Creek and Cabin Creek recently."

At the beginning of the strike there were 55 mines operating on Cabin Creek and 41 on Paint Creek, employing 7,500 miners. Those workers and their families made up a population of about 35,000 people, who lived in the squalid mining camps along the two creeks.

With the exception of the Cabin Creek miners, the whole Kanawha River coal field had been unionized for several

AUTHOR'S NOTE: In those early days of the industry there were no large consolidated mining corporations, and the mines on these two creeks were mostly individually owned by residents of Charleston, or by small companies whose stockholders were also Charlestonians. The Carbon Fuel Company was the largest producer in the district.

years. But for some reason the Paint Creek union miners had been paid two and one-half cents less per ton for mining coal than the prevailing wage at surrounding union mines. In negotiating for a new contract they demanded an increase of this small difference, which would have amounted to about fifteen cents a day for each miner. The operators refused the demand, and a strike was called for April 18, 1912.[1]

Encouraged by the strike of their nearby Paint Creek neighbors, the non-union miners on Cabin Creek submitted the following demands to their employers:

"(a) That the operators accept and recognize the union; (b) that the miners' right to free speech and peaceable assembly be restored; (c) that 'black-listing" discharged workers be stopped; (d) that compulsory trading at company stores be ended; (e) that 'cribbing" be discontinued, and that 2,000 pounds of mined coal constitute a ton; (f) that scales be installed at all mines to weigh the tonnage of the miners; (g) that miners be allowed to employ their own check-weighmen to check against the weights found by company weighmen, as provided by law; and (h) that the two check-weighmen determine all 'docking'[4] penalties."

These demands simply asked for observance by the operators of individual rights guaranteed to miners by State statutes and the Federal and State Constitutions. Nevertheless, the coal barons rejected all demands, and the Cabin Creek miners joined their Paint Creek neighbors in the strike.

That the inhuman practice of blacklisting discharged workers existed among the coal companies as far back as 1912, is conclusively shown by the Report of the Bishop Donahue Committee,[5] which said:

"Letters were laid before the committee purporting to emanate from officials of mining plants (on Paint Creek and

[1] See Charleston newspapers, *Gazette* and *Mail*, of April 19, 1912.
[2] See Appendix I, Note 1.
[3] See Appendix I, Note 2.
[4] See Appendix I, Note 3.
[5] See Appendix I, Note 4.

Cabin Creek), and also from detective agencies warning against receiving into their employ certain miners designated by name. Their physical appearance, in some instances, was minutely described. The reasons alleged for their rejection were one or more of the following:

"(a) That they were favorably inclined to the union, or

"(b) That they were trying to organize a branch of the union, or

"(c) That they disobeyed certain orders made for the general safety, or

"(d) That they demanded a check-weighman.

"It is repugnant to the genius of our institutions and to the ordinary instincts of manhood and humanity to deprive permanently a poor, and often wholly illiterate, fellowman of the opportunity of earning his daily bread for himself, his wife, and his helpless children because he insists on his plain rights and the observance of laws, for example, such as that providing for a check-weighman."

The coal companies obtained these reports on their miners through an elaborate espionage system probably never equaled outside Russia. Their spies were employees of the Baldwin-Felts Detective Agency,[6] who worked with the miners, listened to their conversations, and secretly reported all workers who criticized the management, spoke favorably of the union, or agitated for a check-weighman. Such workers were discharged, and, through the blacklisting system, permanently eliminated from the industry.

In the spring of 1913, Borah's Senate committee investigated the causes of this strike and conditions generally in the affected area. "The Evidence," said the committee in its Report, "showed that the workers complained bitterly against the practice of 'cribbing'.[7] In some instances, it was stated, they were required to load as much as 3,000 pounds for a

[6] See Appendix I, Note 7.
[7] See Appendix I, Note 2.

ton. Housing conditions, too, were bad, the houses being leaky and without resistance to cold, mere frame shanties."[8]

The evidence before the committee also showed that many camps were shockingly unsanitary. In describing such conditions, Adjutant General Elliott, who commanded the troops in the strike zone, testified:

". . . There are employers who encourage the worst forms of degeneracy .... Last year (1912), I visited a filthy mining camp that was in charge of a college graduate. He was a fairly intelligent chap, who thought he had a lot of animals in the village instead of human beings. The houses were dirty, the store was kept in slovenly rot. Outside the store was much decayed matter, and rubbish was everywhere. I ordered the boss to clean up the place. At first he did not seem to understand the order, and I had to go a second time. I said to him: 'If this place is not cleaned up by noon Tuesday I will order my soldiers to burn the village, beginning with the store.' The place was cleaned up in short order."

In summarizing the causes of the strike, Senator Kenyon, of Iowa, expressed them all in two words, "HUMAN GREED."

For nearly a month the strike was conducted without the slightest violence. In the meantime, the operators contracted with the Baldwin-Felts Detective Agency for sufficient mine guards to "break" the strike. On May 10, 1912, the first contingent of guards arrived, bringing with them a number of trained bloodhounds. They continued to arrive in detachments until there were three hundred or more guards on the two creeks.

These guards were professional strikebreakers, all tried on a dozen industrial battlefields, and willing to shoot with or without provocation. They were led by Albert and Lee Felts, brothers of Thomas L. Felts, head of the agency, both killed eight years later in the Matewan Massacre.

Many of these guards were not even residents of the State,

[8] See Appendix I, Note 2-a, for an explanation of the U. S. Senate Borah Committee that investigated the Cabin Creek and Paint Creek strike.

some had criminal records, and a few could boast of at least one "notch" each on their guns. They immediately began a campaign of assault, intimidation, and terrorism without parallel in the history of American industrial struggles.

A group of armed mine guards on Paint Creek.

One detachment of guards was under the direction of the notorious Tony Gaujot (pronounced Go-show), a native of "Bloody Mingo" County.[9] He was a tough old ex-sergeant of the regular army, and holder of the Congressional Medal of Honor. The strikers said that of all guards on the two creeks, "Old Tony" was the most heartless and brutal.

The first move of the operators was to evict all strikers from their company-owned houses. The coal companies owned all the land on both sides of the creeks for a distance

[9]A few years after his guard service on Paint Creek and Cabin Creek, "Old Tony" was shot to death in Williamson, county seat of "Bloody Mingo" County, by his nephew, Jim Gaujot. Jim was sent to the penitentiary, served a few years, and was paroled by the Governor. He was killed a few months later in a plane crash.

of twenty miles or more; and upon their autocratic command the guards loaded the miners' meager household goods into freight cars, hauled them across the boundary line of the company property, and dumped them along the railroad tracks. Other guards, armed with high-power rifles, herded men, women, and children into groups, like so many cattle, and drove them down the valleys and off the company property.

Homeless, hungry, and ragged, the strikers and their families found shelter in caves, tents, and improvised shacks, on privately owned lands. Day and night, month after month, stretching into more than a year, these starving human beings huddled in their filthy and unsanitary quarters, and were fed by the miners' union. The children were denied access to the public schools because they had moved out of their school districts; while the strikers could neither approach the post office nor travel roads on the creeks without permission from the coal operators, because they were on company-owned lands.

In its report to the Governor, the Bishop Donahue Committee[10] that investigated the strike thus denounced the operators' mine guards in the strike zone.

". . .These guards openly and flagrantly violated the rights guaranteed the miners on Paint Creek and Cabin Creek, respectively, by natural justice and the Constitution... the denial of the rights of free speech and peaceable assembly, and the many and grievous assaults on unarmed miners, show that their purpose was to overawe the miners and their adherents and, if necessary, to beat and cudgel them into submission.

"We find the system employed was vicious, strifepromoting and un-American. No man worthy of the name likes to be guarded by others armed with blackjacks, revolvers and Winchesters while earning his daily bread. It is repugnant to the spirit of the laboring man and we believe to the opinion of the American people. We are therefore unani-

---

[10] See Appendix I, Note 4.

Mine guards on Cabin Creek–"Old Tony"
sitting beside machine gun on right.

mously of the opinion that the mine guard system as presently constituted should be abolished forthwith."

But the Legislature took no action, and the mine guards continued to rule the creeks.

In further preparation for the coming storm, the coal companies installed numerous searchlights at strategic places and constructed a number of concrete forts or "pillboxes" at commanding points in the valleys. The most formidable looking of these structures was on Cabin Creek in front of the company buildings of the Carbon Fuel Company. From its portholes, rifles and machine guns could sweep the valleys and mountainsides in all directions.

With their forts in place and surrounded by mine guards, the operators began to reopen their mines with imported scab[11] workers, and that act intensified the bitterness among the strikers. To lure strikebreakers to the fields the operators published false and deceptive advertisements in large eastern papers offering "STEADY EMPLOYMENT AT GOOD WAGES IN THE MINES OF WEST VIRGINIA, NO STRIKES, FREE TRANSPORTATION." The new workers were brought in by special trains, escorted by mine guards; but once in the camps they were virtual prisoners and kept under guard. But as they learned the truth, many escaped at night and joined the strikers. (A number of newspapers containing these advertisements were introduced in evidence before the U. S. Senate committee.)

The operators were led by the late Charley Cabell, known as the "Boss of Cabin Creek," superintendent of the Carbon Fuel Company, largest producer in the district. He was a stoop-shouldered, wiry, domineering, little man, with an unquenchable hatred for the miners' union and an unreasonable distrust of his workers. He rejected all offers of the Governor for a compromise, and ordered a fight to the finish. Of course, he was simply carrying out the orders of the mine owners.

---

[11] "Scab" is a contemptuous term union members apply to non-union workers who take their places during strikes.

The strike leaders were two fiery, dynamic, young miners scarcely out of their teens-Frank Keeney and Bill Blizzard. After this strike ended, they each worked and fought their way to the top of the miners' union in their district. A decade later, they were the central figures in the insurrection known as the "Armed March."[12]

[12] See Chapter 13.

Chapter 3

OLD MOTHER JONES APPEARS

The spark necessary to start the conflagration on the two creeks was furnished by the sudden appearance among the strikers of Old Mother (Mary) Jones,[1] an organizer for the miners' union and idol of coal

Old Mother Jones on Cabin Creek.

miners everywhere. She was an 82-year-old, fiery, fearless, profane, and vulgar labor agitator, who for more than forty years had been a firebrand in American industrial troubles. She possessed no qualities of leadership, but was a sort of gadfly sent out by the union leaders to annoy the operators.

The old incendiary decided to present Governor William E. Glasscock with what she called "a living petition," to urge him to intervene in the strike. Accordingly, she called for the strikers to assemble on the State Capitol grounds on a Sunday afternoon and invited the Governor to attend the rally, but he left the city the day before the meeting.

For possible use in an injunction suit, the operators planted a court reporter in a nearby office who took down the proceedings, including Mother Jones' speech.

[1] See Appendix I, Note 5.

The old agitator addressed the mob of strikers from the front steps of the Capitol. She denounced the Governor in the most violent and vulgar language for "running away." "You can expect no help from such a goddamned dirty coward," she said, "whom, for modesty's sake, we shall call 'Crystal Peter.' But I warn this little Governor that unless he rids Paint Creek and Cabin Creek of these goddamned Baldwin-Felts mine-guard thugs,[2] there is going to be one hell of a lot of bloodletting in these hills." Then she screamed at her listeners: "Arm yourselves, return home and kill every goddamned mine guard on the creeks, blow up the mines, and drive the damned scabs out of the valleys."[3]

With money supplied by the union, the strikers purchased all guns and ammunition in the city stores, ordered a halfdozen machine guns, 1,000 high-power rifles, and 50,000 rounds of ammunition, and returned to their jungle. In the meantime, the operators had converted all company buildings in the valleys into arsenals in which they had stored sufficient arms and ammunition to equip a regiment of soldiers. In short, both sides were rapidly preparing for the gathering storm.

The Governor submitted to both sides a proposition to arbitrate the differences, but it was rejected by the operators. With all hope of a compromise gone and embittered by the wrongs they had suffered, the strikers resorted to the rifle. Armed and desperate, they roamed the mountainsides and picked off mine guards in the valleys below at every opportunity.

The first bloodshed occurred when two Baldwin-Felts mine guards, W. W. Phaup and Robert Stringer, were ambushed and fired upon by strikers. Stringer was killed instantly, and Phaup was shot through the shoulder. The badly wounded guard eluded his assailants in the darkness, and

[2] See Appendix I, Note 7.
[3] In 1925, the late Jess Sullivan, secretary of the West Virginia Coal Operators Association, loaned me a transcribed copy of this speech by Mother Jones. These excerpts were taken from it.

Baldwin-Felts mine guards killed and wounded in strike zone-Top: W. W. Phaup, wounded; Robert Stringer, killed near village of Pratt. Bottom: J. E. Hines, killed in battle of Mucklow; D. C. Slater, killed at village of Eskdale.

made his way through the jungle to the Sheltering Arms Hospital on the mountainside below the town of Montgomery.[4]

The crazed strikers invaded the hospital, bent upon finishing their bloody work; but the doctors told them that the wounded guard had died on the operating table, and showed them the sheet-covered corpse of a man who had died a few hours earlier, and they departed. The following night Phaup was removed to a hospital in Richmond, Virginia, where he recovered. He returned to Bluefield, and took no further part in the strike.[5]

Phaup discarded his blood-soaked coat beside the trail as he struggled to reach the hospital, and it was picked up by his pursuers. At a mass meeting of strikers held the following Sunday at Cabin Creek Junction, Old Mother Jones held up the bloody coat before the crowd and shouted: "This is the first time I ever saw a goddamned mine guard's coat decorated to suit me." She then had the coat cut into small pieces, which she threw to the mob. The strikers, screaming their delight, gathered them up and pinned them to their coat lapels as decorations of honor.

For weeks the witless carnage continued. Assaults, murders, pitched battles, and destruction of property were daily occurrences, while nightly, from wooded mountain slopes, the strikers poured a withering rifle fire into the mining camps.

Both valleys became infernos of blood and hate. Strikers' wives fought beside their husbands with tigerish fierceness, and a few were the victims of such brutal assaults by mine guards that they were delivered of stillborn babies. (Testimony before the Borah Senate Committee.)

The sniping finally culminated in a general battle at the mining camp of Mucklow, on Paint Creek, in which no fewer than 100,000 shots were exchanged by the contending

[4] This hospital was operated as a missionary enterprise by the Episcopal Church for the benefit of miners. It was abandoned and razed many years ago.

[5] Phaup gave me these details personally when he returned to Bluefield.

forces. The village was shot to pieces, not a house escaped, some were shot through as many as 100 times.

The newspapers reported sixteen killed-four mine guards and twelve strikers. This was probably correct as to the guards, but only speculation as to the number of strikers killed, as they carried away their wounded and buried their dead and made no report to the authorities.

However, the climax in the struggle came on September 1, 1912, when the union miners on the north side of the Kanawha River, inflamed by the sufferings of their brethren in the strike zone, armed themselves and crossed the river to aid the strikers. The combined armies, estimated to number 6,000 armed and infuriated men, climbed the mountain, passed through the woods overlooking the coal camps, and massed on the ridge at the headwaters of Cabin Creek. Their avowed purpose was to march down the creek, "kill every goddamned mine guard, destroy all coal tipples, and drive the goddamned scabs out of the valleys," as ordered by Old Mother Jones.[6]

As to conditions in the strike district at that time, and the immediate necessity for drastic action by the State, the aforementioned Bishop Donahue Committee said in its Report to the Governor:

". . .these strikers saw red, and, with minds bent on havoc and slaughter, marched from Union District across the river, passed through the woods overlooking the creek and mining plants, finally massing on the ridge at the headwaters and arranging to swoop down Cabin Creek and destroy everything to the Junction.

"Meanwhile, the operators hurried in over a hundred additional heavily armed guards, purchased several deadly machine guns and many thousands of rounds of ammunition. Several murders were perpetrated and all who could, got away; men, women, and children fled in terror and many hid in cellars and caves. If ever there was a case for strong meas-

[6] See Charleston newspapers, *Gazette* and *Mail*, of August 31, September 1, 2, and 3, 1912.

ures like martial law, the conditions prevailing on Monday, September 1, 1912, the eve of the martial law proclamation, presented it ....

"We believe,... that but for the martial law proclamation taking effect when it did, there would have been great destruction of property and loss of live in the strike zone. The enormous quantities of rifles, revolvers, and other weapons, including machine guns, captured from both sides and brought to the military camp at Paint Creek Junction, also bore mute, but eloquent, witness of the height to which the passions of the opposing forces had mounted."

In the meantime to oppose the invading army of strikers and their sympathizers, the mine guards, reinforced by all store clerks and bookkeepers who could fire a rifle, had mobilized to resist the invasion. Barricades were hastily constructed, breastworks thrown up, and machine guns mounted at strategic points, behind which 400 determined defenders awaited the onslaught.

Such was the situation on the morning of September 2, 1912, when the Governor declared the entire strike district under martial law, and 1,200 state militia, who had been converging on Paint Creek and Cabin Creek all night by special trains, were rushed into the territory.[7]

[7] See Charleston newspapers, *Gazette* and *Mail*, of September 2 and 3, 1912.

Chapter 4

MARTIAL LAW

At first, the strikers hailed martial law with delight. The soldiers disarmed the mine guards, sent some to jail and drove the others from the district.[1] Two machine guns and 15,000 rounds of ammunition consigned to one coal operator[2] were seized at the express office and returned to the consignor.

Rifles, machine guns, pistols, and ammunition seized by the militia in the strike zone. Boxes on left contain 225,000 rounds of machine gun ammunition.

Both operators and strikers were ordered to hand over their arms and ammunition. During the first few days of military rule 1,872 high-power rifles, 556 pistols, 6 machine guns, 225,000 rounds of ammunition, 480 blackjacks, and a

[1] When they left the Cabin Creek and Paint Creek areas, the Baldwin-Felts mine guards were sent to Colorado to help break the strike of the coal miners against the Colorado Fuel and Iron Company. The union charged that these guards led the vicious attack on the strikers' tent colony at Ludlow, Colorado, in which eleven women and two children were killed. (See *Universal Encyclopedia*, volume 5, page 1864.)

[2] The term "operator" means *mine owner*.

large number of daggers, bayonets, and brass knuckles were surrendered to or seized by the soldiers. But most of the rifles and four of the machine guns were given up by the operators. The strikers were skeptical. While a number turned in their weapons, the majority hid them with friends outside the military zone.

But the iron hand of military rule soon fell heavily upon the strikers. Under the Governor's proclamation no "congregating" of the miners was permitted. A military court was set up at the village of Pratt and a nearby freight house converted into a temporary jail, which the strikers called the "Bull Pen." All military prisoners were held in this stockade until their cases were disposed of by the military court.

A few days after the martial law proclamation, at the village of Eskdale, on Cabin Creek, Mother Jones undertook to read the Declaration of Independence to a group of strikers at the railroad depot. A couple of young militiamen grabbed her by the arms and hustled her down the creek. But the old lady maintained that she had a constitutional right to read the Declaration of Independence anywhere at any time. "Hell's fire," said one of the young guardians of the peace, "was that what you was readin'? I thought you was incitin' a riot. But we have orders to lock you up anyway," and she was taken to the Bull Pen but soon released.

Under the first martial law rule, 66 persons were tried and convicted of various offenses. In most cases short jail sentences were imposed, but a few strike leaders were sent to the penitentiary for long terms. These summary proceedings had a sobering effect upon the strikers, and by October 15, 1912, the disturbances had quieted down to the extent that the Governor lifted martial law, and the militia departed.[3]

Freed from active military duty, many soldiers accepted employment with coal companies as guards and became the protectors of the imported scab miners. Inflamed at seeing their old jobs taken by others, while their wives and children starved, the strikers brought their rifles out of hiding, and

[3] See Charleston newspapers, *Gazette* and *Mail*, of October 16, 1912.

early in November the war was resumed with greater violence than before.

The soldier-guards were even more brutal than the Baldwin-Felts strikebreakers, and the strikers fought with the grim desperation of men who were starving. The mining camps and the trains bringing scab workers into the district became the constant targets of such murderous rifle fire from the mountainsides that, by the middle of November, the strikers were in full control of the riverfront of the strike zone, and refused to permit trains to operate on the creeks.

Militia encampment on Paint Creek.

On the evening of November 15, the Governor issued his second martial law proclamation, and special trains rushed the militia back into the strike district. The soldier-guards left their company employment and rejoined their respective commands. Thereafter, the military forces ceased to be the impartial arbiter between the coal companies and the strikers, and began a determined effort to crush the miners under the iron heel of military might.[4]

[4] See the Charleston newspapers, *Gazette* and *Mail*, of November 16, 1912.

A second military court was set up, which not only took cognizance of offenses committed within the strike district during the second military occupancy, but also assumed jurisdiction of all offenses committed within the area during the interval when martial law did not exist.

The strike area embraced less than one-tenth of the county. The county's civil courts were open and functioning as usual. Yet, the military tribunal usurped the functions of the civil courts within the strike district, and civil authorities even arrested persons outside the martial law area and turned them over to the military courts for trial.

There may be just complaint against the cumbrous machinery and interminable delays of courts of law; but no such accusation could be made against the military tribunals that ruled the destinies of Paint Creek and Cabin Creek. Men were arrested one day, tried the next, and sent to the penitentiary the third. The rights of prisoners to counsel of their own choosing and to stand mute before their accusers were disregarded. The practices of the long-dead Spanish Inquisition were revived, and prisoners were forced to give evidence against themselves. The right of prisoners to separate trials was wholly ignored—as many as thirty having been tried together. Long penitentiary sentences were imposed for offenses which the law defined as misdemeanors, punishable by small fines.

In civil life the judges of the military courts were laymen, many of whom did not know the difference between a felony and a misdemeanor, and their judgments reflected their lack of knowledge. In testifying before the Borah Senate Committee, the members of the various military courts admitted under oath that in pronouncing their judgments they were not "controlled by any law, either human or divine"; that they did not consider themselves "bound or restrained" by the provisions of either the State or Federal constitutions; and that penalties prescribed by State law for various offenses were wholly ignored.

A number of victims of the military courts were brought from the penitentiary to testify before the Borah Senate

Committee. Among them was S. F. Nance, who was convicted for an alleged offense committed in the interim between two successive periods of martial law. In part his testimony was (Quotation marks omitted):

Senator Martine:	Were you sent to the penitentiary?
Mr. Nance:	Yes, sir.
Senator Martine:	You were tried before whom?
Mr. Nance:	The military court.
Senator Martine:	On what charge were you arrested?
Mr. Nance:	Interfering with an officer.
Senator Martine:	Was that charge true?
Mr. Nance:	(Condensed) After the first martial law was lifted, and before the second proclamation, I got into an argument with a soldier at the railway station. No licks were struck. We just had a cussing match. My wife and I were leaving for Kentucky. I was gone about ten days. When I got back martial law had been declared again.
Senator Martine:	Who arrested you?
Mr. Nance:	General Elliott.
Senator Martine:	Did he serve a warrant on you?
Mr. Nance:	He just walked up and took me by the arm and said: "I want you."
Senator Martine:	Did he read a charge to you?
Mr. Nance:	No sir. He took me and locked me in the Bull Pen.
Senator Martine:	How long were you in this pen?
Mr. Nance:	Two nights. I was arrested on Tuesday, tried on Wednesday, and sent to the penitentiary on Thursday.
Senator Martine:	What was your sentence?

Mr. Nance:	Five years.
Senator Martine:	Did you have any witnesses?
Mr. Nance:	I gave them the names of four witnesses, but they did not call them. I didn't have any witnesses. (*Senate Record*, pages 190-1.)

A number of other prisoners testified along the same lines, and no witnesses were introduced to contradict them.

Again, the iron rule of military might was triumphant; cowed strikers hid their rifles and went back to their tents and caves; the operators brought in their scab workers under military protection; the mines resumed operations; and thousands of men, women, and children starved. "Law and order" were restored to the extent that on January 10, 1913, the militia was withdrawn and martial law died without a formal proclamation suspending it. But, as before, a number of soldiers remained behind as private mine guards for the coal operators.

Chapter 5

THE BULL MOOSE SPECIAL

In the meantime, to protect the imported workers as they were transported up the strike-torn creeks, the Chesapeake and Ohio Railroad ordered its Huntington shops to prepare an armored train, as near bulletproof as possible. But when the union shopmen learned its purpose, they stopped work on it. However, after the railroad officials assured them that the train was to be used only as a mail carrier, and its armor was for the protection of the crew and mail clerks against stray bullets, they resumed work on it and completed the job.

This train, known locally as the "Bull Moose Special," consisted of a locomotive, baggage car, and day coach— all protected by heavy steel plates. The railroad company permitted the operators' mine guards to equip it with the instruments of death. A machine gun projected menacingly from each side door of the baggage car, and a number of highpower rifles and an ample supply of ammunition were kept in the day coach. Notwithstanding the assurances given the shop workers by railroad officials, the train was used to transport scab workers up the two creeks.

On the night of February 7, 1913, Boner H. Hill, Sheriff of Kanawha County, six of his regular deputies, and fourteen mine guards headed by Quinn Morton, a Paint Creek coal operator, boarded this train at Charleston for the Paint Creek strike zone. The Sheriff's purpose was to serve a warrant sworn out by Morton for the arrest of that aged and elusive, but always culpable, criminal, "John Doe," whom the coal man charged with "inciting a riot."[1]

As the darkened train moved into the tent village of the strikers at Holly Grove, which was strung out along both sides of the railroad track, the machine guns began spitting

[1] See Charleston newspapers, *Gazette* and *Mail,* of February 8, 1913.

fire and death; and the coal operator and his mine guards opened fire with high-power rifles from the car windows. Sleeping miners and their families awoke in the middle of the night to hear bullets ripping through their tents and shacks. A few strikers returned the fire with rifles, while screaming women and children fled into the wintry night, clad only in their scanty night clothes. One miner was killed and a few wounded. But the Sheriff neither ordered the shooting, nor did he or his deputies participate in it. It was the exclusive "party" of the coal operator and his mine guards.

Lee Calvin, a mine guard on the train, testified before the U. S. Senate Borah Committee, that, after this nocturnal expedition of death had passed through the village, the coal operator remarked, apparently to all those in the car: "We gave them hell and had a lot of fun. Let's back up and give them another round." But the Sheriff refused to permit it, and denounced the shooting as a wanton act of barbaric cruelty.

When this evidence was detailed before the Senate Committee, Senator Martine, of New Jersey, angrily exclaimed:

Senator Martine:	"This man, who in the name of heaven can he be, who would propose to go back and kill more? Is he an ordinary citizen?"
Mr. Jackson:[2]	"He will be before you, Senator."
Senator Martine:	"Well, God help us all then."

In his testimony, the coal operator denied that he made the remark, as stated by Calvin, but admitted that Calvin was in the coach throughout the trip. He also admitted that he repeatedly fired a high-power rifle into the tent village. He refused to answer the following question asked by Senator Martine:

---

[2] This was the late Malcolm Jackson, counsel for the coal operators.

"I want to ask you whether you deem it a civilized method to use a machine gun on helpless women and children?"[3]

In 1947 former Sheriff Hill wrote me that when he began the trip he had no idea that shooting would occur; that the shooting lasted less than two minutes; that when it was over the coal operator did make the remark testified to by witness Lee Calvin; and that he refused to permit the train to "back up," and denounced the shooting. He also stated that, when the shooting began, he was standing in the aisle looking through a window, and the flashes from the guns fired from outside were very plain, and he "firmly believes the first shots came from outside firing at the train."

On February 10, 1913, three days after the attack on Holly Grove, the Governor issued his third martial law proclamation, and again troops were rushed into the strike district.[4] The Bull Pen was reopened, a new military court convened, and 166 strikers were brought before it for trial. A few were acquitted, many given jail sentences, and a score or more sentenced to long terms in the penitentiary, including Old Mother Jones who was convicted of "inciting a riot" and sentenced to twenty years in prison.

In the meantime, on the first Wednesday in January, 1913, the Legislature convened at the State Capitol in Charleston, less than twenty miles from the strike district. A few days after the Holly Grove incident, the lawmakers and residents of the city were thrown into a panic by the report that 5,000 armed and infuriated strikers were mobilizing for a march on the Legislature and the City of Charleston. The families of a number of coal operators hurriedly left town; the Mayor armed around two hundred special police officers; and two companies of militia were rushed from the strike zone and thrown around the Capitol building; machine guns were set up at commanding points, and all persons (including this writer) entering the Capitol grounds were searched for arms and explosives. But the strikers abandoned the march, and the excitement gradually subsided.

---

[3] See Report of Borah Senate Committee, pages 846-7, and 964-5.
[4] See Charleston newspapers, *Gazette* and *Mail*, of February 11, 1913.

Chapter 6

RAPE OF THE CONSTITUTION

By the inclusion of Sections 4 and 12 of Article III of the State's Constitution,[1] its framers, no doubt, believed that they had locked every door against military tyranny. But these military courts not only ignored these guaranties, they also denied their victims the protection of the Fourteenth Amendment to the Constitution of the United States, in that the defendants were deprived of their liberty without "due process of law."

This "due process clause" means that citizens accused of crime are entitled to be tried in accordance with the established rules of evidence, customs and usages guaranteed by the laws and constitutions of the State and the United States. This having been denied the military prisoners, they were deprived of the "equal protection of the law" guaranteed by the Fourteenth Amendment to the Constitution of the United States.

Two victims of the military courts sought their release from the penitentiary in *habeas corpus* proceedings before the State's Supreme Court.[2] To the amazement of the country, that Court upheld their conviction on the theory that a statute authorized the Governor "in the event of invasion, insurrection, rebellion, or riot," to "declare a state of war." But a statute that contravenes the Constitution is void.

It is a far cry from this decision to the great pronouncement of the Supreme Court of the United States in *Ex Parte Milligan*, 4 Wall. 121. In that case, during the Civil War, a military court in Indiana tried, and sentenced to death, a man named Milligan for treason against the United States. The civil courts of the state were open and functioning, just as they were in Kanawha County during the strike, and, for that

[1] For these two sections of the State's Constitution, see Appendix I, Note 6.
[2] See *Mays and Nance vs. Brown, Warden*, 71 West Virginia Supreme Court Reports, page 519.

reason alone, the Nation's highest judicial tribunal held that the military court was without authority in the case.

"The Constitution of the United States," said the Court, "is a law for rulers and people, equally in war and in peace, and covers with the shield of its protection, all classes of men, at all times, and under all circumstances. No doctrine involving more pernicious consequences was ever invented by the wit of man than that any of its provisions can be suspended during any of the great exigencies of government. Such a doctrine leads directly to anarchy and despotism."

But the West Virginia Supreme Court was not unanimous in its decision. Judge Ira E. Robinson refused to yield his judicial honor to the usurpation of the Governor, and his dissenting opinion deserves to rank as a great landmark in the age-old struggle against military tyranny.

In brief, the dissenting Judge said that the Constitution provides that "'... no citizen... shall be tried or punished by any military court for any offense cognizable by the civil courts of the State'; and only the annihilation or inoperation of the civil courts of Kanawha County could create the necessity that would legalize these military courts; and that the mere proclamation of the Governor, setting aside a small area within the county as a martial law district, could not create such necessity.

"The proper civil courts of the county were open and functioning as usual," continued the dissenting jurist. "The petitioners could have been tried there, by a jury, upon an indictment by a grand jury. If necessary, the militia could have transported them out of the disturbed area to the seat of the county government for trial, just as they were transported to the penitentiary after their conviction by the military court. Hence, no necessity existed for thus supplanting the civil authority by the military court.

"The only excuse offered for the failure to try petitioners in the civil courts is that the Governor ordered otherwise. Thus the Governor made the necessity. But the Governor may not set aside constitutional guaranties. Therefore, the trial and sentence of the prisoners were not by 'due process of law,' and were grossly illegal and void."

But the opinion of the majority of the Court prevailed, and the will of the Governor became the "Supreme Law of the Land" in the strike district.

A side result of the Supreme Court's decision was to affirm the conviction and 20-year sentence of Mother Jones. At the time, I was engaged in a month's legal work in Charleston and I decided to visit the village of Pratt, observe the military court in session, and, if possible, talk with Mother Jones before her removal to the State prison.

At the Pratt railway station, a young soldier informed me that the military court would not be in session that day, but he pointed out a little two-room shack near the Bull Pen in which Mother Jones "was held under guard." As I neared the shanty, I found my way barred by a bayonet attached to a rifle in the hands of a lad in military uniform. He advised me that the only way I could see Mother Jones was to bring a written order from the Governor.

On my way back to the depot I met Captain George M. Ford, who commanded a company of militia in the strike zone. I had known him for several years, and frankly told him why I was there. "It is the Governor's orders," said he, "that no one be permitted to talk to the military prisoners; and we must carry out those orders to the letter.

"By the way," the Captain continued, "a half hour ago our soldiers had to shoot a striker up on the creek, and all hell is liable to break loose here any minute. Should trouble start, you will be safer in the railway station; and when the train comes you had better get back to Charleston."

As I rode the train back to the State's Capital, over and over again I asked myself: "Can this be America?" But that was more than fifty years ago.

Conditions in the strike areas continued to grow worse until March 4, 1913, when the late Dr. Henry D. Hatfield took office as Governor, succeeding William E. Glasscock. Hatfield was an eminent physician and surgeon—a native mountaineer who possessed all the physical courage of his feudist kinsmen of an earlier day.

The new Governor decided to investigate personally the entire strike situation before approving or disapproving the many pending convictions of the military courts, which his predecessor had left for him to pass upon. Disregarding the advice of the military authorities, that the bitterness of the strikers was such that he might be killed, shortly after daylight the morning after his inauguration, he left the Executive Mansion, alone, with his medicine case in hand, and, a short time later, stepped off the train in the village of Pratt, in the very heart of the strike district.

The Governor's first professional call was at the shack that served as the temporary prison of Old Mother Jones. He found her lying on a straw tick on the floor, ill with lobar pneumonia, with a temperature of 104 degrees, and without a nurse or medical attention. To prevent the escape of this aged and helpless "criminal," and thus further endanger the safety of the coal operators and their properties, a young soldier-guard, carrying a loaded rifle with fixed bayonet, paced with measured tread, back and forth, in front of her shanty door.

As commander in chief of the State's military forces, the Governor ordered Mother Jones' guard withdrawn immediately; that she be removed on the first train to her room in the Fleetwood Hotel in Charleston[3]; and that nurses and a competent physician be provided for her. His orders were carried out, and the aged patient quickly recovered. However, she was still a military prisoner and could not return to the strike district.[4]

In the meantime, still anxious to meet and talk with Mother Jones, I changed to the Fleetwood Hotel and was assigned a room quite near hers. In time, we became acquainted, and she talked freely about the strike and her arrest

---

[3] The Fleetwood Hotel was on the west side of Capitol Street a short distance south of Fife Street. It is now a mercantile establishment.

[4] In the summer of 1960, former Governor Hatfield gave me the details of this incident.

and conviction. Her old eyes twinkled as she described her arrest for reading the Declaration of Independence to a group of strikers. "The tragedy is," said she, "the young boys who arrested me had no knowledge of that immortal document, and no conception of its meaning."

"I knew the goddamned operators were after me," she said, "and, while I encouraged the miners to continue the fight, I never violated a single military order. But the coal barons' military court held that, in addition to crimes committed in the strike district after martial law was declared, it also had jurisdiction of offenses committed within the area before the martial law proclamation—a sort of *ex post facto law*. I was convicted because of the speech I made at Cabin Creek Junction three months before the first martial law declaration—the time we cut up that goddamned mine guard's bloody coat and gave the pieces to the strikers. But, I am not afraid. Governor Hatfield is an honest man, and the operators can't bully him. He will never stand for such injustices."

The Governor spent two days in the strike zone, treating the sick, consoling the bereaved, and creating goodwill wherever he went. But the operators resented his presence on the creeks. They said that he was "toadying to the damned strikers." A few days later they unwisely sent to the Governor a delegation of operators, headed by Charley Cabell, to protest against any further conciliatory efforts by him. Their second mistake was in assuming that they could continue to give orders to the new Governor, as they had to his predecessor. Cabell began by sharply questioning the wisdom of the Governor's visit to the strike area. Quickly, the Governor gave him a clout on the side of his head that sent him sprawling into a corner, and then ordered him from the office.[5]

[5] My last talk with the late former Governor Hatfield was in the summer of 1960. I mentioned this incident, and said: "Doctor, if it is true, I would like to include it in my book." He replied: "It is true. I did lose my temper, which a Governor should never do. I regret it very much."

Governor Hatfield was a nephew of Devil Anse Hatfield, leader of his clan in the noted Hatfield-McCoy Feud.

Turning to the rest of the delegation, the Governor said: "Gentlemen, you are not giving the orders now, you are taking them. This madness has got to stop. The State's general taxpayers have already contributed more than a million dollars to keep troops in your strike-torn coal fields, and they are tired of it. If you and your workers can't agree on the terms of a settlement, then I shall dictate the terms, and both sides will accept them. I will give you a few days to try to settle this strike with your employees."

The Governor rejected the majority opinion of the Supreme Court, and agreed with the dissenting jurist that every citizen charged with crime has a constitutional right to a trial by a jury in the civil courts. He disapproved all pending sentences of the military courts, including the conviction of Mother Jones, paroled all military prisoners sent to the penitentiary and various county jails before he assumed office, and served notice on the operators that their brutality toward their employees must stop.

As was expected, the operators and union leaders were unable to agree, and the Governor dictated the terms of peace, forced both sides to accept them and, in four weeks, brought to an end the most disastrous labor war in the history of the State.

With the Governor's aid the strikers won a partial victory, but at a tragic cost in privation, hunger, suffering, and death. The Paint Creek miners gained the niggardly two and one-half cents a ton increase in wages; the Cabin Creek workers won recognition of their union; and for a few years both operators and miners employed their own check-weighmen at the mines; and the workers on the creeks secured a temporary respite from compulsory trading at company-owned stores.

Thus peace came to these "Valleys of Slaughter."

In the summer of 1965, for the first time in thirty years, I drove the entire length of both Cabin Creek and Paint Creek. It was a sickening experience. A few small mines, employing a mere handful of men, were still trying to operate. But the large coal camps, where fabulous wealth once poured from the mines, are now desolate ruins—coal and people gone, landscapes cluttered with skeletal tipples, empty storerooms, decaying houses with windows and doors gone, deserted churches with roofs sagging and steeples held aloft only by a few rusty nails. Scores of these old tumble-down shacks were occupied, rent free, by forelorn and destitute former miners who existed on "handouts" from the Federal and State governments.[6]

Both valleys are pictures of "Voiceless Woe."

[6]In the summer of 1967 I again visited the two valleys. The only noticeable change was that death had removed a few of the elderly from the relief rolls.

Part Three

THE VALLEY OF THE TUG

The Tug is the left fork of the Big Sandy River, and for a distance of 75 miles it is the boundary line between West Virginia and Kentucky. Two West Virginia counties lie mostly within its basin—Mingo, toward its mouth; and McDowell, within its upper reaches. Since the early 1890's, both counties have been large coal producers. In 1920-21, the valley was torn by the State's bloodiest labor war, and on two occasions during the strike the President sent U. S. Army troops into the district to quell the disorders.

Chapter 7

BLOODY MINGO

Mingo County was created by the West Virginia Legislature in 1895 by bisecting Logan County. It is a land of high mountains, deep gorges, rushing streams, and blood feuds. But the coming of the railroad in 1892 and the development of the coal industry replaced the feuds with violent labor wars, and the guns that once blazed in the feuds were used later in those wars.

From earliest times, the inbred contempt of many Mingo mountaineers for the law and their disregard for human life earned for the county the unenviable sobriquet of "Bloody Mingo." Even in more recent years opposing political factions have frequently "shot out" their differences on highways and village streets. In 1934, the newspapers reported that Circuit Judge B. F. Howard, in appealing from the bench for an orderly election in the town of Williamson, referred to the county as the "hell hole of creation."

These mountaineers always speak of peace officers as "The Law," and sometimes their dislike for The Law extends to the highest echelons of officers. A few years ago two gunmen waylaid James Damron, Circuit Judge of the County, and fired a few pistol slugs into his body, and left him for dead. The Judge recovered, but his murderous assailants were never apprehended.

In 1925, citizens of the village of Kermit divided into two hostile factions over the creation of an independent school district. On election day (May 19) they decided to let bullets and not ballots decide the issue. More than two hundred shots were fired in the battle, and when the smoke cleared, two men lay dead, two were desperately wounded, and a few had flesh wounds.[1]

---

[1] The principal of the village school was the late Floyd E. Morris, one of my college friends and an active supporter of the school plan. A few months after these killings, Morris told me that he had been marked for death, but was saved by an accident. A few minutes before the shooting he had left the voting place and gone to his residence for some election supplies, and when he heard the shooting his wife locked the doors and they stayed inside the remainder of the day. Both Charleston newspapers, *Gazette* and *Mail*, of May 20, 1925, carried an account of this battle.

But the county's most brutal wholesale killings occurred in the evening of May 19, 1920, on the main street of the crime-ridden village of Matewan, and grew out of a strike of coal miners. The incident is remembered as the "Matewan Massacre."[2]

The Mingo County operators said that Sheriff Blankenship proposed to them that, for the payment to him of a sizeable cash sum, he would prevent any union activities in the county during his term of office, and they rejected the proposal. Thereupon, said the operators, the Sheriff began negotiations with the miners' union. What he received, or whether he received anything, is unknown. But shortly thereafter the union began to organize the miners in the county.

Supported by the Sheriff, Mayor Testerman of Matewan, and "Two-Gun" Sid Hatfield, village Chief of Police, the union called a strike at Red Jacket and other mines near Matewan village to force the operators to recognize the newly organized union. But the unrest soon spread to other sections of the county, and eventually developed into a major labor war. As usual, the strikers and their families were fed by the union.

Finally, the Red Jacket Company decided to evict certain strike leaders from their company-owned houses. It secured eviction writs from a justice of the peace in an obscure sec-

----

[2] The statements in this chapter about the Massacre, and also those in the next succeeding chapter about the trials of defendants, are based upon the following:

1. Stories related to me by surviving mine guards, Oscar Bennett, Bill Salter, G. A. Anderson, and J. R. Anderson, all of whom lived in or near Bluefield.

2. Statements made to me by an eyewitness to the Massacre, Dr. Wade F. Hill, and also upon the transcript of his testimony given at the first trial of the killers.

3. The complete transcript of the testimony given at the first trial, loaned to me by Capt. Ruel E. Sherwood, one of the court reporters in the trials.

4. My attendance at the Court during the last three days of the first trial, when I heard the closing arguments to the jury by counsel for both sides.

5. News stories in the *Bluefield Daily Telegraph*, beginning May 20, 1920, the day after the Massacre, and continuing for a week. Also news stories in the same paper, beginning the first day of the first trial, January 10, 1921, and continuing throughout its nine-week duration.

6. See also statement of Judge Robert D. Bailey, who presided at both trials, as set out in Appendix I, Note 8.

tion of the county and turned them over to the Baldwin-Felts Detective Agency for execution.[3]

This Agency, with headquarters in Bluefield, was a ruthless, strikebreaking organization headed by William G. Baldwin and Thomas L. Felts—the two most feared and hated men in the mountains. For more than thirty years its employees, called "Baldwin Thugs" and mine guards by the workers, had ruled the coal fields, fought strikes and strikers, and otherwise tyrannized over the miners.

On May 19, 1920, a posse of twelve of these mine guards, led by Albert and Lee Felts, brothers of Tom Felts, one of the owners of the Agency, left Bluefield by train to carry out the eviction orders. Only four guards, the Felts brothers, Bill Salter, and C. B. Cunningham were licensed to carry pistols. The others carried high-power rifles, for which no license was then required.[4]

There was no demonstration when the guards arrived in Matewan. They went to the camp, evicted the strikers, returned to the village, cased their rifles, and were standing about the street waiting for the train on which they expected to return to Bluefield. Everything appeared serene, but it was the calm of death.

Chief of Police Sid Hatfield passed Albert Felts on the sidewalk and shot him through the head while Felts' back was toward him. Apparently that was the signal for the massacre to begin; and, from second story windows and other vantage points, a deadly rifle and pistol fire was poured into the mine guards. Five guards, including Lee Felts, brother of Albert, fell dead from the first volley.

Salter and Cunningham, who had pistols, opened fire on their assailants. His pistol empty, Salter ran through a store

---

[3] See Appendix I, Note 7.
[4] The rifle-carrying guards were G. A. Anderson, J. R. Anderson, R. C. Buchanan, all of Bluefield, Oscar Bennett, of Bramwell, J. W. Ferguson, a former policeman of Princeton, all of West Virginia; and C. T. Higgins, a former policeman of Galax, A. J. Boorher, a former policeman of Bristol, and E. O. Powell, a former policeman of Marion, all of Virginia.

Top—Circles on buildings indicate bullet holes and scars of the battle.
Bottom—Main Street of Matewan where Massacre occurred.

and hid in a large wastepaper container on its back porch until the middle of the night, and then swam Tug River to Kentucky and safety.[5]

---

[5] A few months later, Salter was one of the killers of Sid Hatfield and Ed Chambers on the courthouse steps at Welch. See Chapter 9.

Cunningham was the last guard to fall. Although mortally wounded by the first volley, he propped his fast-failing body against a lightpole and emptied his pistol at the attackers. With his pistol empty, his knees buckled, and he slumped to the sidewalk. "Two-Gun" Sid Hatfield slunk from the shadows and fired a few pistol balls into the dying man's head, and then nonchalantly remarked to the mob: "That goddamned son-of-a-bitch sho had a heap o' guts."

The unarmed guards who survived the first deadly fusillade, some desperately wounded, fled in every direction. J. W. Ferguson, badly wounded, ran into a nearby house and hid under a bed; but two killers rushed in, jerked the bed aside, seized the dying man by the feet, dragged him into the street, and fired a number of pistol slugs into his body. Oscar Bennett saved his life by slipping into the railway station and mingling with the passengers waiting to take the train. The two Andersons and Buchanan ran through a store and down the railroad tracks toward Williamson and escaped.

The battle over, seven guards, Mayor Testerman, and Robert Mullins and Tot Tinsley, two striking miners, lay dead in the street; and three strikers and a bystander were seriously wounded.

Whether true or not, the miners believed that over the years many strikers had been wantonly killed by the Baldwin-Felts mine guards. No other organization was so bitterly hated by them; and here were two of the chief offenders, Albert and Lee Felts, of Cabin Creek and Paint Creek infamy, and five of the lesser ones lying dead at the feet of their conquerors. The mob's hatred became wild fury; and passengers on the train that pulled into the station a few minutes after the battle was over were horrified to see the bodies of ten dead men lying where they had fallen, here and there in the street near the depot, and a howling, jeering, shrieking mob, led by Chief of Police Sid Hatfield[6] and Ed

---

[6] In 1925, the late H. S. (Sol) White, a former State Senator and a resident of Matewan for many years, told me that Sid was not actually a Hatfield, but that he was raised by a respectable family named Hatfield, and just assumed the name of his foster parents.

Chambers, dancing around the bodies and spitting tobacco juice into the glassy eyes of the dead mine guards.

A few jars of "moonshine" whiskey were brought out of hiding and the frenzied killers drank greedily. For hours the drunken mob held "high carnival with death" over the bodies of the dead mine guards, and fired hundreds of bullets into their lifeless forms. Skulking ghouls, the lowest of human thieves, robbed the dead of all money, jewelry, and other valuables. The high-power rifles and ammunition belts were added to the arsenal of the strikers, but Chief of Police Hatfield stole the pistols of the dead Felts brothers. As the night wore on, the drunken mob became weary and gradually disappeared, and undertakers from Williamson were allowed to claim the bodies of the dead mine guards.

Later, at the trials of the murderers, Tom Felts testified

Baldwin-Felts mine guards killed in Matewan Massacre—Top: C. T. Higgins, Albert Felts, and Lee Felts. Bottom—C. B. Cunningham, A. J. Boorher, E. C. Powell, and J. W. Ferguson.

that when on "assignment" his brothers always carried large sums of money for use in emergencies; that when they left his office in Bluefield for Matewan each brother was given $1,000 in cash for use in any emergency that might arise; that each brother wore a very valuable 2-carat diamond ring; that their bodies were robbed of the money and the rings; and that neither the money nor the rings were ever recovered.

Mayor Testerman had a beautiful young wife for whom the amorous Chief of Police, Sid Hatfield, had formed a passionate attachment, which was reciprocated by the "lady fair." After the massacre it was generally believed in Matewan that Hatfield had planned the whole affair to give him an opportunity to remove the Mayor from the triangle—and that he did so remove him.

Be that as it may, the "grief-stricken" widow married the village Lothario seven days after the funeral of her "very late" husband. Also, the night before the wedding, the two were arrested by police in the City of Huntington for prematurely occupying the same bed. On a table beside their bed were the pistols of the dead Felts brothers. They were seized by the police and returned to the Baldwin-Felts Agency.

As usual, the officials of the miners' union tried to justify these murders and also undertook to make a hero out of the chief murderer—Sid Hatfield. They employed a small moving picture company to make a silent movie called "Smilin' Sid." It showed local mining camps; strikers' tent colonies; groups of striking miners with their ragged and hungry-looking wives and children; a gruesome reenactment of the Massacre; and Sid Hatfield, with a moronic grin on his pasty face, brandishing a large-caliber pistol in each hand.

The picture was shown in several union camps, and finally reached Mercer County, home of the Baldwin-Felts Agency. Sheriff B. B. Hunt feared that its showing might precipitate a riot between mine guards and union sympathizers, and notified the theater owner at Princeton that the picture could not be shown in the county. While they were discussing the matter, a Baldwin-Felts detective, dressed in the uniform of an

Top—Union relief day at Matewan. Bottom—A
flying squad of Mingo militia.

expressman, entered the office, delivered a fake package,
and, unnoticed by either the Sheriff or the theater owner,
walked out with the "Smilin' Sid" film. Two years later, when
the public had lost all interest in the picture, the film was
expressed to the theater owner from Cincinnati, Ohio, by an
unknown party.[7]

---

[7]   I was Prosecuting Attorney of Mercer County at the time of this
incident and the details were reported to me by Sheriff Hunt.

Chapter 8

THE MOCK TRIALS[1]

Sid Hatfield and twenty-two other participants in the Massacre were indicted for the murder of the seven mine guards. The killers and union leaders knew that unfriendly witnesses had to be silenced. In most cases fear sealed their lips. With others, a simple warning was sufficient to convince them that they saw nothing.

But Anse Hatfield, a hotel keeper in Matewan, was of a different breed. He was a bold, courageous, truthful mountaineer, who could neither be bluffed nor intimidated. He had witnessed the slaughter, and would tell exactly what he saw. But he could be silenced. One afternoon, shortly before the trial date, as he sat smoking on his hotel porch, a rifle cracked on the nearby mountainside, and Anse Hatfield slumped to the floor, a bullet through his head. The perpetrator of that foul murder was never apprehended.[2]

Trial day finally arrived, January 28, 1921. The city of Williamson, county seat of Bloody Mingo, seethed with excitement, and its people were fearful. They knew that a street battle was imminent. Many of the local residents stayed off the streets, and business places in the vicinity of the courthouse did not open on the first day of the trial.

The evening before the trial was to begin, fifty picked and heavily armed State Police moved into the city. The following morning they took up advantageous positions in and around the courthouse. The same morning two score of the toughest of the Baldwin-Felts mine guards, loaded down with guns, suddenly appeared and lounged here and there about the streets, alert and expecting trouble.

Promptly at nine o'clock the Judge rapped his gavel for order. As Court opened, the closing sentence of the Crier,

---

[1] See Appendix I, Note 8.
[2] The details of this murder were told to me by the late Senator H. S. (Sol) White, a long-time resident of the village of Matewan.

"God save the State of West Virginia and this Honorable Court," sounded ominous. The first case called for trial was that of Sid Hatfield and twenty-two co-defendants for the murder of Albert Felts, and they elected to be tried together. But as the trial progressed, seven of the defendants were dismissed for lack of evidence connecting them with the shooting.

On the third morning, Court officials and attorneys were thrown into a panic by the report that 1,000 armed mountaineers, members of the union, were mobilizing for a march on the courthouse to protect the prisoners from the "Baldwin Thugs," as these mine guards were called by the miners.

To avert possible trouble, the Judge called a conference of attorneys and union leaders. A union mountaineer informed the Court that the report was correct. "Jedge," he drawled, "we think them thar Baldwin Thugs are here to do away with our men if they are acquitted. If shootin' starts, we ain't aimin' to come out second best. If them thar Baldwin Thugs will leave town, our men will go back home, and we'll let jestice take its course."

A truce was arranged. The mine guards left town, the miners returned to their homes, and the trial proceeded.

To the consternation of defendants, they were soon confronted by two surprise witnesses—Dr. Wade F. Hill and Everett Lively. No doubt, Dr. Hill had saved his life by keeping silent, and the strikers had long regarded Lively as one of their number.

As a young dentist, Dr. Hill had opened his office in Matewan a year or two before the killings. He testified that his office was on the second floor over a store, and looked out on the town's main street; that a few minutes before the shooting he closed his office, went down the steps, and as he stepped out of the doorway he saw Albert Felts standing on the edge of the sidewalk, with his back toward him, talking to a man whom he did not know, and who stood in the street in front of Felts; that he also saw Chief of Police Sid Hatfield approaching from the right; and, just as he came even with

Felts, Hatfield jerked a pistol and fired directly at the back of Felts' head, at very close range; that Felts crumpled to the sidewalk, and instantly the firing became general from many positions; that he ran into a store behind him, and stayed there until the shooting was over; that he then went back upstairs to his office and stayed there through the remainder of the night; and that from his office window he watched the wild orgies of the killers as they robbed and mutilated the dead.[3]

After his testimony, Dr. Hill knew that for him to remain in Matewan meant death. So he moved to the town of Logan

Defendants in Matewan Massacre trials—Left to right (standing): Jim Maggard, foreman of jury that acquitted defendants, Reece Chambers, C. H. Kisser, Fred Burgraph, Sid Hatfield, Nat Atwood, Ed Chambers, Lee Toller, and Clare Overstreet. Left to right (kneeling): Bouser Coleman, Ben Mounts, Bill Bowman, Van Clay, Art Williams, and Hallie Chambers.

[3] Dr. Hill's evidence was corroborated by the four guards who survived, and also by a dozen strangers who were waiting at the station to take the train.

in an adjoining county, where he practiced his profession until his death in 1947.[4]

As a secret agent of the Baldwin-Felts Agency, Lively had gone to Matewan and opened a restaurant three weeks before the Massacre, and remained there until the first trial. His place became a rendezvous for strikers, and he was their associate and confidant. They repeatedly detailed to him how they had planned the slaughter, and described the part each defendant had played in it.

The trial lasted nine weeks, the longest murder trial in the State's history. But, notwithstanding the conclusiveness of the evidence, it was a judicial farce and its results a foregone conclusion long before it began. Every member of the trial jury well knew that the safety of his home and property, even his life, depended upon his recorded vote of "not guilty" for all defendants; and each juror so voted.

In a discussion of the two Massacre trials, during a visit to his office on June 27, 1961,[5] Judge Bailey told me that the defense testimony in those trials was a tissue of the most fantastic falsehoods he ever had to listen to during his years on the bench.

In brief, defense testimony was that Albert Felts tried to get Mayor Testerman to permit the mine guards to mount at least a couple of machine guns on the flat roofs of two of the town's most strategically located buildings, and the Mayor refused; that Felts then told the Mayor that he had a warrant for the arrest of Chief of Police Sid Hatfield, and he was going to take him to Williamson for a hearing before a justice; that the Mayor replied that if Felts had a warrant for Sid he might arrest him, but he, the Mayor, would hold the preliminary hearing in Matewan. Thereupon, said the defendants and their scores of perjurers, Felts jerked a pistol and shot the Mayor; that instantly Chief Hatfield shot Felts, and the

---

[4] Dr. Hill's wife and my wife were first cousins. I knew him intimately, and he related the story of the Massacre to me on at least three occasions.
[5] See Appendix I, Note 8.

shooting then became general; but in every case the mine guards were shooting at the defendants, and they shot only in self-defense.

Its secret operatives reported to the Baldwin-Felts Agency that the Massacre was instigated and planned by Reece Chambers, his son Ed, and Chief of Police Hatfield, and the mine guards decreed that this trio must die.

Reece Chambers lived in the narrow valley of the Tug a short distance above Matewan, and his home was within easy rifle range from passenger trains of the Norfolk and Western Railroad. A year after the Massacre, Hughey Lucas, a notorious Baldwin-Felts mine guard, told me that for months after the killings, a trusted Baldwin-Felts man and a dead shot, made frequent trips on the train, always occupying a drawing room on the side next to Chambers' house; and that as the train neared his residence, the would-be killer would raise the window a few inches, rest the muzzle of his rifle on the window sill, and peer through the telescope sight for his intended victim. But danger had made the elder Chambers cautious, and he missed death by not venturing from his house when a train was passing. But his son Ed and Sid Hatfield were not so fortunate. Their end is written in blood on the steps of McDowell County Courthouse.[6]

Seven mine guards died in the Massacre and the killers still faced six indictments for murder. However, it was common knowledge that any jury of Mingo County citizens would be afraid to convict them, no matter how strong the evidence. Under the State's Constitution only a defendant may ask for a change of venue (transfer of his case to another county for trial); and it was certain that these killers felt perfectly secure among their own kind, and would never ask for a venue change. Thus it appeared that the State was completely blocked in its efforts to bring these criminals to justice.

In January, 1921, however, the Legislature enacted a general law which authorized any judge to summon a jury from another county whenever he deemed such action necessary.

[6] See Chapter 9.

Immediately, the Circuit Judge of Mingo County ordered a jury from Pocahontas County to try the defendants. When Court opened, an attorney for the prosecution stated to the Court: "I now find it necessary to advise the Court officially that two of the defendants, Sid Hatfield and Ed Chambers, have come to an untimely end; and I ask that the indictment be dismissed as to them." And it was done.

The remaining defendants elected to be tried together, upon an indictment charging them with the murder of mine guard J. W. Ferguson. After a trial that lasted seven weeks, the jury failed to agree on a verdict and was discharged. It stood eleven for conviction of murder in the first degree, and one for acquittal. All remaining cases were continued until the next term of court. Further continuances were had from time to time; but, eventually, all indictments were dismissed.

It was the general opinion at the time that the juror who voted "not guilty" had been bribed by an agent of the miners' union before he left Pocahontas County.

Chapter 9

McDOWELL COUNTY'S RETRIBUTION

From the time the coal industry began to be developed within its borders in the early 1890's until the miners were unionized under the New Deal Legislation of the Roosevelt Era, climaxed by the Wagner Act of 1935, McDowell County was a complete industrial autocracy, with every branch of the county government and every phase of the lives of the people dominated by a super-oligarchy of coal operators. During those years, too, its law enforcement officers were employees of the aforementioned Baldwin-Felts Detective Agency.[1]

Those employees were strong-armed thugs, called *mine guards*. Usually, two such guards, duly commissioned as deputy sheriffs by the county authorities and paid by the coal companies, were stationed at every mining camp in the county. Their purpose, said the operators, was to preserve law and order in the camps. The truth is, they were there to keep union organizers out of the county. Their slogan was: "Nobody ever killed a Baldwin-Felts man and lived very long to brag about it."

One night, shortly after the first Massacre trial in Williamson, the mining camp of Mohawk in McDowell County, a short distance from the Mingo County line, was "shot up." The mine guards said that this shooting was done by Mingo County strikers, led by Sid Hatfield and Ed Chambers, to force the Mohawk miners to join the union.

The union leaders countered that the shooting was done by McDowell County mine guards, who then falsely accused Hatfield and Chambers of the offense. The purpose, said the union leaders, was to force them to come into McDowell County to answer the charge—a place where they could be summarily and safely dealt with according to mine guard justice. In the light of subsequent events, this theory was undoubtedly correct.

---

[1] See Appendix I, Note 7; also Appendix III, Story of Keystone.

Thomas L. Felts, active head of the Baldwin-Felts Detective Agency,
the most feared and hated man in the mountains.

Be that as it may, Hatfield and Chambers were indicted in McDowell County for the offense. A day was fixed for them to appear in court, give bond, and have their cases set for trial. Sheriff Bill Hatfield (no relation to Sid) assured counsel for defendants that their clients would have the fullest protection of his office.

August 1, 1921, was the fateful day.[2] The train carrying Hatfield and Chambers on their one-way ride from Matewan pulled into the depot at Welch. Apparently, all was peaceful, but farther up the street the stage was already set for the "dance of death." Sheriff Bill Hatfield, who had promised defendants' protection, had left the county the day before to "take the waters" at Craig Healing Springs, Virginia.

On the courthouse lawn a deadly reception committee of Baldwin-Felts mine guards, all McDowell County deputy sheriffs and sworn to preserve the peace, was in line to receive the visitors. This committee was headed by "Buster" (George) Pence, Bill Salter,[3] and Everett Lively[4]—a trio of deadly gunmen. Flanking them on either side were a half dozen other mine guards, all heavily armed and equally deadly; while inside the ivy-covered courthouse the wheels of mountain justice (?) were slowly turning.

Hatfield and Chambers, with their newly wedded wives, and C. J. Van Fleet, a union attorney from Pittsburgh, went to the hotel and secured rooms. Later, Van Fleet said that Chambers was unarmed, and at his suggestion, Hatfield left his gun in his hotel room, where it was found after the killings. As they were leaving the hotel, Van Fleet was called back to answer a long distance telephone call, which probably saved his life.

The two killers, accompanied by their wives, swaggered slowly up the street toward the courthouse, as ignorant of

[2] See *Bluefield Daily Telegraph*, August 2, 1921, and subsequent issues.
[3] Salter had saved his life at the Massacre by hiding in a wastepaper container until the middle of the night and then swimming Tug River to Kentucky.
[4] This was the same Everett Lively who, as a Baldwin-Felts secret agent, opened a restaurant in Matewan three weeks before the Massacre.

the deathtrap into which they were walking as had been the Baldwin-Felts mine guards at Matewan a few months earlier. They climbed the steps to a platform, from which there was a right-angled turn and more steps leading up to the level courthouse yard. From the platform they looked up into the cold, merciless eyes of Pence, Salter, and Lively—eyes burning with hate.[5]

Instantly, the trio of guards began firing, while the notorious mine guard, Hughey Lucas, turned and fired a number of shots against the stone wall of the courthouse to make it appear that Hatfield and Chambers were armed and had fired first at the mine guards, but missed. About a year later Lucas told me that he emptied his pistol against the courthouse wall.

Pierced by four bullets, Hatfield fell lifeless from the grasp of his frantic wife, while Chambers, shot three times, pitched headlong down the steps and lay still. He, too, was dead. Miraculously, the wives were unhurt. The shooting over, Hatfield's wife fled screaming through the smoke into the courthouse, while Chambers' wife sank to the sidewalk and sobbingly pillowed her dead husband's head in her lap. Immediately, a dozen mine guards formed a cordon around the bodies and prevented all spectators from approaching. Two guards forcibly led the hysterical Mrs. Chambers' from the bloody scene. But she soon returned. No guns were about the bodies when she was led away, said the widow, but, when she returned pistols were clenched in the dead hands of the murdered victims. "Buster" Pence's old and often repeated self-defense racket of "Kill 'em with one gun, and hand 'em another one," had been worked again.[7]

---

[5] Query: Welch was Detachment Headquarters for the State Police. Why did they fail to protect the Mingo County criminals?

[6] Mrs. Ed Chambers later married Harold Houston, attorney for the miners' union. During the winter of 1942-43 I was a neighbor of the Houstons in Lake Worth, Florida. I talked with Mrs. Houston a number of times about the murder of her former husband. And I have recorded here the facts and circumstances of the tragedy just as she related them to me.

[7] See Appendix I, Note 9.

Top—left, "Two-Gun" Sid Hatfield; right, Ed Chambers. Bottom—Courthouse at Welch. The "X" marks the spot where Hatfield and Chambers died.

But, even in McDowell County, the formalities of the law had to be satisfied. Then, too, future county authorities might not be so friendly toward mine guards. To prevent any possible future prosecution of the killers, it was necessary to have a jury's verdict of "acquittal" for all defendants in both killings. Therefore, Pence, Salter, and Lively were duly indicted for the murder of both Hatfield and Chambers. Why Lucas[8] and the other guards who were present aiding and abetting in the killings were not indicted was never explained.

These brutal killings had been witnessed by a number of citizens of Welch, but fear sealed their lips; and the defendants were promptly acquitted on the grounds of self-defense. Thus was "justice" dispensed (with) in the coal-controlled county of McDowell.

A few months after the acquittal of the trio, the late Judge I. C. Herndon, a resident of Welch, and then Judge of the Circuit Court of both McDowell and Mercer counties (not the court in which the guards were tried), told me that he was convinced "that the whole thing from the 'shooting-up' of the Mohawk camp to the killing of Hatfield and Chambers, was a well-laid plan of the Baldwin-Felts mine guards and certain county officials to get the Mingo criminals into McDowell County where the guards could safely take summary vengeance for the Matewan killings."

"Judge," I said, "under the law, you had the authority to call a special grand jury in your court to investigate these killings. Why didn't you do it?"

"Because," said he, "I knew that it would be impossible to get a grand jury that was not controlled by the coal operators and mine guards. I also knew that if I started an investigation I would be killed before a grand jury could assemble, and I was not ready to die to avenge the murder of two such notorious outlaws as Sid Hatfield and Ed Chambers."

This conspiracy theory is strongly supported by still another circumstance.

A few months after the mine guard trials at Welch, the

---

[8] Two years after the Welch trials, the notorious Hughey Lucas became involved in an illicit affair with the wife of a miner at Montcalm, Mercer County, and was shot and killed by the irate husband.

Mercer County officers arrested a McDowell County "shine runner" with fifty gallons of moonshine whiskey in his car. He had purchased the liquor in the moonshine region of "Shootin' Creek," Virginia, and was running it through to McDowell County. He asked his captors to take him to my office (I was Prosecuting Attorney) so he could call a bondsman from his county.

He placed a long distance call for one of McDowell's most prominent coal operators. While waiting on the call, I said to him:

"Mr. -- is a very busy man. Why do you think he will bother with you?"

"He will either come or send someone," he replied. "You see, I am not a bootlegger. This liquor was for a few of the 'big shots.' Then, too, I was on the jury that acquitted the Baldwin-Felts men for killing Sid Hatfield and Ed Chambers. Any of the operators will help me."

"Your jury service sounds interesting. Tell me about it," I said.

"There ain't much to tell," he replied. "About a week before the trial date, a deputy sheriff came to me and said: 'If you were called on the jury to try the Baldwin-Felts men for killing Sid Hatfield and Ed Chambers, how would you vote?'

"By God! I'd vote 'not guilty,' I told him.

"The deputy then pulled a blank summons for jury duty out of his pocket, wrote my name on it, and handed it to me."

"Did you serve on either jury?" I asked.

"Yes, on the jury that tried them for killing Sid Hatfield, and we all voted 'not guilty.'"

"Were the other jurors selected the same way you were chosen?" I asked.

"Sure they were," he replied.

At this point the prisoner talked to the coal operator, and then said to me:

"He will send a bondsman immediately."

And he did.

In 1937, a few months after the death of Tom Felts, I said to a prominent resident of Welch for more than thirty years:

"Now that both Tom Felts and Bill Baldwin are gone, their detective agency no longer in existence, and people may express their opinions without fear, what is the general opinion of the people of Welch respecting the killing of Sid Hatfield and Ed Chambers?"

"Among those who are familiar with the facts," he answered, "the opinion now is the same as it was when the killings occurred—that they were carefully planned and deliberately carried out by the mine guards, with the connivance of certain county officials. And it is likewise believed that the trials of the killers were judicial farces, staged for the sole purpose of acquitting them."

Of the twenty-three indicted killers, Sid Hatfield and Ed Chambers, victims of private vengeance, were the only ones who paid the extreme penalty for their part in the Massacre. And it is still widely debated among the people of the mountains whether or not the mine guards, in their role as vigilantes, were justified in the summary execution of those two notorious criminals.

Chapter 10

WAR ON THE TUG

The Matewan Massacre was only the beginning of a long train of violence in the Tug Valley which the State was unable to suppress. Its militia had not been reorganized since World War I, and the small number of State Police could not cope with the situation.

Over the protest of the Sheriff, the County Court appointed 800 special deputy sheriffs, and the Circuit Court licensed them to carry pistols. This volunteer police force, called "Mingo Militia" by the strikers, soon allied itself with the mine guards, which intensified the bitterness among the strikers.

After their eviction from company-owned houses, the strikers set up "tent colonies" along Tug River, and were fed by the union. But many supplemented their meager ration by making "moonshine" whiskey and selling it to the thirsty non-striking miners.

On June 14, 1920, a group of the newly appointed deputy sheriffs attacked a strikers' tent colony. One striker was killed, food supplies were destroyed, and a number of tents cut to pieces.

That wanton act precipitated the "Three Days' Battle of the Tug," between 2,000 strikers on one side, about 1,000 deputy sheriffs and mine guards on the other side, in which more than 200,000 shots were exchanged. Which side started the battle is uncertain, for both sides were armed and seemed anxious to "shoot it out." For three days the battle raged intermittently along an eight-mile front, and only with the exhaustion of their ammunition did the strikers abandon the fight and silently disappear into the jungle.

The mining camps of Merimac and McCarr were in the battle zone. In the former, the wives and children of nonstrikers huddled inside the mine for safety; and, in the latter, they found refuge in the basement of the company store. A baby was born at McCarr with mattresses piled high around the bed as a protection against bullets.

The casualties in the battle were never known. The strikers buried their dead and carried away their wounded, and the opposing side refused to make any statement. However, Squire Staton, who would have been one of the State's chief witnesses in the Massacre trials, was killed on the second day of the battle.

While the battle was in progress, the Governor appealed to the President for Federal troops to suppress the disorders. The day after it ended, a regiment of regular army troops entered that "Death Valley" of the coal fields, restored a semblance of order, and was withdrawn in three weeks.

In the meantime, on March 4, 1921, E. F. Morgan was inaugurated Governor, and the "War on the Tug" was renewed with increased violence. The new Governor declared the strike district under martial law, and sent Major Tom B. Davis, Acting Adjutant General of the State, into Bloody Mingo to enforce his proclamation.

"A state of war, insurrection, and riot is, and has been for some time, in existence in Mingo County," said the proclamation, "and many lives and much property have been destroyed as a result thereof, and riot and bloodshed are rampant and pending." Even freedom of the press was suspended. "No publication," continued the decree, "either newspaper, pamphlet, handbill, or otherwise, reflecting in any way upon the United States, or the State of West Virginia, or their officers, may be published, displayed, or circulated within the zone of martial law."

His experience as a satrap on Paint Creek and Cabin Creek, during the bloody strike years of 1912-13, had amply qualified Major Davis for the task of enforcing martial law along the blood-stained waters of the Tug, but the efficiency of the system had greatly improved since those dark days.

The Major's first order was to forbid all persons to enter the tent colonies of the strikers, unless they lived therein, and also to prohibit all assemblages within the strike zone. But

Fruits of a "still hunt" in strike district-1. Judge R. D. Bailey, who tried defendants in Massacre trials; 2. Major Tom B. Davis, who enforced martial law in Mingo County.

this last order was enforced only against strikers and their sympathizers. Business in the valley went on as usual; people continued to assemble at church services and picture shows, as had been their custom; but if two strikers started down the valley they had to keep a lonesome distance between them.

Without warrants, civil officers and the Mingo Militia arrested strikers for violation of the Major's orders, and brought them before him for trial. He was lawmaker, judge, and jury. Warrants or other formal complaints were regarded as superfluous, and even the formalities of a trial by courtmartial were dispensed with as being unnecessary red tape. The Major's autocratic will was law, and within a few days he had imprisoned more than one hundred persons in the county jail for violating his arbitrary orders.

To liberate these prisoners and to end what the miners

Strikers' tent colonies in the strike district.

called the "Despotic Reign of the Emperor of the Tug" were two objectives of the miners who joined the Armed March.[1]

However, a union organizer named Lavender obtained his release from jail in a habeas corpus proceeding before the State's Supreme Court.[2] "Martial law cannot exist," said the Court, "where the State fails to employ its military arm to enforce it." This ruling ended the Major's authority on the Tug and liberated all his prisoners.

The Governor then asked the President for immediate military aid in suppressing the disorders, and special trains rushed 1,000 battle-equipped army troops into the strike district; and for months the narrow valley of the Tug echoed to the tread of Uncle Sam's Regulars.

There were no further organized disorders in the valley— just a murder or two every few days.

---

[1] See Chapter 13.

[2] See *Ex Parte, Lavender*, 98 West Virginia Supreme Court Reports, page 713.

Chapter 11

THE YELLOW-DOG CONTRACT

The most far-reaching outgrowth of Bloody Mingo's labor wars was the development and use of an innocent-looking, legally binding, politically explosive, little written agreement that soon became stigmatized throughout labor circles by the opprobrious name of "Yellow-Dog Contract." It was even so designated in dignified Congressional debates. It acquired this scurrilous title because miners were compelled to sign it in order to secure or hold employment in the mines.

These contracts differed somewhat in language at the several mines, but in substance and effect they were all the same. The one given here was taken from the Court records in the Red Jacket Case, hereinafter mentioned.

CONTRACT OF EMPLOYMENT[1]

I am employed by and work for the _____ Company, of , West Virginia, with the express understanding that I am not a member of the United Mine Workers of America, and will not become so while an employee of said _____ Company; that said Company agrees to run an "Open Shop" while I am employed by said _____ Company. If at any time I want to join or become connected with the United Mine Workers of America, or any affiliated organization, I agree to withdraw from the employment of said Company, and I further agree that while I am in the employ of said Company that I will not make any efforts amongst its employees to bring about the unionization of said employees against the Company's wishes. I have either read the above or it has been read to me.

Dated this the _____ day of _____, 19_____.

(Signed)

---

[1] This contract is almost identical with that used by the *Hitchman Company* in the case hereinafter discussed. It is styled *Hitchman Coal & Coke Company vs. Mitchell, et als.* 245 U. S. Supreme Court Reports, page 229; 62 L. Ed. page 260.

This little contract proved to be the most powerful weapon ever devised for excluding the miners' union from West Virginia's coal fields, and, strange as it may seem, it was supplied to the operators by the union itself. If the union had not violated its union contract with the *Hitchman Coal & Coke Company*, and had it not tried to induce that company's workers to break their individual contracts of employment, there would not have been any *Hitchman Case*; and if there had been no *Hitchman Case*, there probably would not have been any Yellow-Dog Contract in West Virginia.

In view of the incalculable influence that this *Hitchman Case* had in shaping the later decisions of our lower courts, and the tremendous impact those decisions had upon the industrial and political life of the country, a brief review of the history of that celebrated case seems timely.

In addition to its mine in Marshall County, West Virginia, the Hitchman Company also owned and operated a mine in Ohio. Certain coal areas, known to the trade as the Central Competitive Field, embraced western Pennsylvania, Ohio, Indiana, and Illinois—but not West Virginia. That Competitive Field, including the Hitchman Ohio mine, was unionized. The West Virginia territory, including the Hitchman Marshall County mine, was nonunion.

In April, 1903, the union told the Hitchman Company that unless it unionized its West Virginia mine, the union would call a strike at its Ohio mine and close it. Thus coerced, the company agreed to the unionization of its West Virginia mine.

In 1906, there was a general strike in the Competitive Field, and, although there were no grievances at the Hitchman West Virginia mine, the union, in violation of its contract, called out its miners in a sympathy strike.

The union did not provide these strikers with sufficient relief funds, and seven weeks after the strike began the hungry miners sent a committee to the company officials to inquire under what terms the miners could return to work. The company had decided to operate its mine nonunion, and the strikers were told that they could return to work only as nonunion miners and after they had signed individual contracts of employment. The strikers accepted the terms, signed the contracts of employment, and the mine resumed operations as a nonunion mine.

The union, however, began to pressure these workers to breach their contracts, return to the union, and continue the strike. On October 24, 1907, the Hitchman Company filed its petition in the U. S. District Court asking for an injunction to prohibit all such union activities, and a temporary injunction was awarded. The union appealed the ruling, and the case was bandied about in the courts upon appeals, rehearings, and rearguments until December 10, 1917 (ten years), when the U. S. Supreme Court decided the case in favor of the Hitchman Company and awarded it a permanent injunction against the union.

Immediately following the Matewan Massacre, the Red Jacket Coal Company, in Mingo County, required each of its nonunion miners to sign individual Yellow-Dog Contracts. Basing its petition on the rule of law laid down in the *Hitchman Case*, the company then instituted an injunction suit in the U. S. District Court to restrain the United Mine Workers of America, its agents and members, from interfering with the company or its employees in the operation of its mines. This procedure was quickly followed by all other coal companies in Mingo County.

On March 31, 1922, the operators in the New River field refused to renew their contracts with the miners' union, and declared for the "open shop." The union called a strike throughout the area. Thereupon, these operators also entered into Yellow-Dog Contracts with their miners who were willing to work nonunion. Backed by these contracts, they also instituted injunction suits in the U. S. District Court to restrain the union from interfering with the operation of their mines.

In all, 231 coal companies instituted these injunction suits; but the cases were consolidated and injunctions awarded in each case. The Court's order prohibited the miners' union and the individual defendants from:

"(1) Trespassing upon or in any manner injuring or destroying the properties of plaintiffs.

"(2) Interfering with employees of plaintiffs, or with men seeking employment in their mines; and from inciting, inducing, or persuading plaintiffs' employees to break their contracts of employment.

"(3) Contributing funds or sustenance to aid the striking miners. . ."

The union carried the cases to the Circuit Court of Appeals, which affirmed the judgment of the District Court in an opinion written by Judge John J. Parker, of North Carolina, and a further appeal to the Supreme Court of the United States was denied by that tribunal.[2]

Based upon identical contracts, the State Courts awarded similar injunctions to 85 coal companies in Mercer, McDowell, and Wyoming counties.

The effect of these injunctions was to isolate perpetually 50,000 coal miners in southern West Virginia, and make it a crime for them to join their union, or for the union to receive them as members, or even to give their striking, starving members a crust of bread.

This was not a law that could be repealed by the State Legislature, or even by Congress. It was a judge-made law from which there was no relief, and that wrote on the lintel of every mine portal in southern West Virginia the Dantesque phrase: "All hope abandon, ye who enter here."

The political repercussions of Judge Parker's decision were no less amazing than its economic results. In 1931 President Hoover sent that jurist's name to the U. S. Senate for confirmation as an Associate Justice of the Supreme Court of the United States. His high legal attainments and exceptional personal character eminently fitted him for the position.

But, notwithstanding the fact that his Red Jacket decision

[2] See *United Mine Workers vs. Red Jacket Company*, 18 Fed. Rep. (2nd Series), page 839.

was based upon a previous holding of the U. S. Supreme Court, which it was his duty to follow, and was later sustained by that High Court, organised labor everywhere began a bitter fight to prevent his confirmation. It was urged that his views on economic and labor problems, as reflected in his Red Jacket decision, "disqualified him for a position that so intimately affects the welfare and industrial liberty of a great people."

The powerful Senators Borah, of Idaho, and Norris, of Nebraska, led an unjustified, but successful, fight against Judge Parker's confirmation in the Senate, and he was rejected 41 to 39.

Although the miners' union in southern West Virginia was dead, the Yellow-Dog Contract was soon to become a far-reaching political issue in the State. In 1930, the late James Elwood Jones, a reputed millionaire and vice-president and general manager of one of the State's largest coal companies, secured the Republican nomination for the United States Senate. At the time, not even his most intimate friends knew that for years his company had operated under the Yellow-Dog Contract system. But the Democrats lost no time in bringing the dusty court records into the spotlight and making it the burning issue in the bitterest campaign ever waged in the State.

As the contest progressed, every branch of organised labor joined in the fight against the Republican candidate, while the coal operators either welshed on Jones or were unable to control their miners as formerly, and he was overwhelmingly defeated. Thus labor took its revenge on one of the originators of what Senator Borah declared was the "most unconscionable contract in our industrial history."

Regardless of the failure of Judge Parker to attain the Supreme Court or James Elwood Jones to reach the United States Senate, Yellow-Dog Contracts and injunctions still barred the way to the unionization of West Virginia's coal miners; and they continued to do so until all miners were unionized under the New Deal Legislation of the Roosevelt Era, beginning in 1933.

As a bitter aftermath of those strikes, Yellow-Dog Contracts, and injunctions, in the years between 1920 and 1925, no fewer than 50,000 men, women, and children were evicted from their homes in southern West Virginia. They found shelter under cliffs, in tents, and in improvised shacks built by the union. Year after weary year they lived and starved in those unwholesome surroundings. Malnutrition and unsanitary conditions increased the death rate to appalling figures, especially among the children. But there was no relenting by the coal barons. To many of them their hungry, protesting workers were pariahs or outcasts, who had to be starved until hunger forced them to return to the service of their masters.

In the end, hunger won, and the workers slunk back to the mines with hearts filled with hate and minds embittered by the memory of the wrongs they had suffered.

Part Four

THE "KINGDOM OF LOGAN"

Logan County was created by the Virginia Assembly in 1824, and embraced nearly nine hundred square miles. On the south it bordered on the Tug and Kentucky, and was named for Chief Logan, who ruled over the Mingo Tribe of Indians. In 1895, the West Virginia Legislature divided it into two counties of about equal size. The northern portion retained the name Logan, and the southern section was named Mingo.

The whole county is a land of tumbled and twisted mountains, deep gorges, and turbulent creeks. Its narrow roads curve dangerously as they wind over the crests and around the slopes of towering ridges, and up the canyons to the mining camps. The inhabitants reside in these deep, narrow valleys, and depend upon the coal industry for a livelihood.

Chapter 12

A "CZAR" RULES THE MOUNTAINS

Logan County is in itself a great coal empire—one of the richest soft coal areas in the world. It lies almost entirely within the watershed of the Guyandotte River, which flows into the Ohio River at the city of Huntington.

To tap that vast coal reservoir, in 1904, two thin lines of steel rails crawled slowly up the winding river into the mountain jungle. The territory developed rapidly, and for years Logan has been the State's largest coal-producing county.

In 1964, Logan County razed its old courthouse and erected a modem structure on the site. Theretofore, in approaching Logan Town, seat of the county government, one could see in the distance the dome of the old courthouse rising above the squat two-and-three-story buildings. On its apex, solitary and dreaming, stood the Goddess of Justice, her eyes blinded as though she refused to look upon the many bloody deeds done in her name in Logan County.

From the time the coal industry began to be developed within its borders, until the enactment by Congress (1933) of the National Industrial Recovery Act, commonly known as NRA, the county was a leer in the face of liberty, a feudal barony defended by soldiers of fortune in the pay of mine owners. To its industrial overlords the miners' union was a nightmare, and to exclude it from their domain they exercised a suzerainty over the county government and suspended the constitutional guaranties of free speech, free press, and peaceable assembly.

At one time the union had subjugated the State as far south as the Kanawha River and New River fields, but it was unable to cross Blair Mountain, the bleak barrier that divides the Guyandotte River and Coal River basins. That abrupt halt in its southward march was due to the relentless opposition of the late Don Chafin, a mountain feudal lord to whom every coal operator in the county paid tribute, and of whom every miner within its borders stood in abject fear.

Chafin was a native of Logan County, born in 1887. The school's records show that he entered the preparatory department of Marshall College (now Marshall University) at the age of 15 and remained two school years. He did no college work and did not graduate. He went to the town of Logan in 1904, when he was 17 years old, and grew up with the town. He was a short, stockily built, dark complexioned mountaineer, who rose to leadership among his kind by native shrewdness and cunning. In his heyday, when clothed with official power, he was a hard-drinking, swaggering, bragging, bullying gunman, who ruled his "Kingdom of Logan" with a mailed fist.

Don Chafin (marked X) and a group of his company-paid deputy sheriffs, known as mine guards.

During his reign, Logan County was overwhelmingly Democratic, with Chafin the BOSS. He was elected county assessor in 1908, at the age of 21 years. This was followed by his election as county clerk, and two four-year terms as sheriff, an intervening term as sheriff being held by his brother-inlaw—with Chafin in control.

While still county clerk, he replaced the Baldwin-Felts mine guards with his own newly organized crew of "peace officers." And, after he became sheriff, he tightened his stranglehold on the county by increasing his deputy-mineguard force to as many as three hundred men. The county records show that during his second term as sheriff, from January 1, 1921, to December 31, 1924, Chafin appointed and dismissed a total of 457 deputies; but the records do not disclose the maximum number on active duty at any given time.

As a further defense against a union invasion, the "Czar," from time to time, had justices of the peace appoint scores of "special constables" and authorize them to carry pistols.[1] These pseudo-officers strutted around, wearing tin badges, and carrying big pistols conveniently holstered under their arms—ever ready to do their master's bidding. These two groups constituted what the miners derisively called the "Standing Army of Logan."

It was openly talked in Logan that the Czar had converted one room of the courthouse into an arsenal in which he kept scores of pistols and high-power rifles, and a half-dozen machine guns, all ready for instant use.

Thus entrenched, Chafin soon became so powerful that he controlled the county government and dominated every phase of the lives of the people. The late E. T. England, the State's Attorney General, and a resident of Logan for many years, openly and repeatedly charged that trial juries were packed with Chafin's henchmen, and a circuit judge and prosecuting attorney compelled to do his bidding;[2] that his evil tentacles enveloped the public schools, and even held the churches in the grip of financial fear; that no school teacher was employed without his approval, and none retained who

---

[1] The custom of appointing and arming "special constables" was carried over into the administration of the next two succeeding Republican sheriffs—Tennis Hatfield and his brother, Joe Hatfield.

[2] I heard Mr. England make this statement more than once. He also made it publicly in his argument before the State's Supreme Court in *Hatfield vs. Scaggs*, hereafter cited. It was not challenged by any member of the Court.

incurred his displeasure; and that at his direction financial support was withheld by coal companies from all churches whose ministers dared to criticize the intolerable conditions in the county.

In some instances, declared the Attorney General, those who dared to oppose the Czar's edicts were ordered to leave the county; and to ignore the warning sometimes meant death, or serious injury, at the hands of his deputy-thugs, who always killed their man in self-defense, or while the victim was resisting arrest, or attempting to escape.

Attorney General England also charged that Chafin maintained his political supremacy in the same way that he kept the miners' union out of his county—by force and violence. In some precincts, the night before election day, the Czar's deputies arrested and jailed Republican election officers on trumped up charges, and filled their places on election morning with Chafin Democrats; and if a precinct was largely Republican, it was not allowed to open, or the ballots were seized and burned after they had been cast.[3]

During the early years of Chafin's rule, there were no roads in the county, and the only means of ingress and egress was by railroad. He guarded his domain against union organizers by keeping one or more of his deputy-gunmen at every railway station. It was openly charged that when a stranger got off the train he was approached by these "merry gentlemen," who demanded to know his name and business in the county. If the replies were not satisfactory, he was told to get back on the train and leave the county. If he refused, he was arrested and taken to the county jail as a "vagrant." If he resisted arrest, he was sometimes soundly beaten and his limp form tossed back on the train, to be carried out of the county, more dead than alive.

A number of such beatings were reported in the press during Chafin's reign in Logan County, but I had personal

[3] For a judicial discussion by the Supreme Court of West Virginia of Logan County's election frauds, see the case of *Hatfield vs. Scaggs*, 101 West Virginia Supreme Court Reports, page 425.

knowledge of only one such incident. J. L. (Tobe) Heiser, Chief Clerk in the State Department of Mines and also a high state official in the Knights of Pythias Lodge, went to Logan Town on an official visit to the local lodge, and to assist in the initiation of a class of candidates. As he entered the town, he was stopped by a couple of Chafin's deputy-thugs who demanded to know his name and his business in the county. Heiser unwisely replied: "That is none of your business." Thereupon, the thugs dragged him from his car, beat him with blackjacks until he was unconscious, and left him lying by the roadside. Some passersby took him to a hospital.

Of course, the story of this brutal attack upon a prominent State employee and a high official of the Pythian Lodge soon appeared, under lurid headlines, in the State's newspapers, followed by highly denunciatory editorial comments. One newspaper ended its scathing editorial with the question: "How long, Mr. Governor, must an outraged public put up with the brutalities of this Logan outlaw and Czar of a selfish coal oligarchy?"

The Logan operators were much disturbed by this unfavorable publicity, and Chafin sent an emissary to Heiser to effect a settlement and quiet the affair. I never discussed the settlement with Heiser, but it was freely talked around the State House at the time that Chafin paid his doctor and hospital bills and gave him $1,000 as compensation for his injuries.

Two stories were current as to how Chafin met the expense of maintaining his feudal army: (a) that he collected from the operators ten cents for each ton of coal mined in the county; and (b) that he collected a certain amount for each deputy employed, paid them a less sum, and kept the difference. But whatever the method, Chafin accumulated a fortune during his reign as the boss of Logan County. In 1921, before the U. S. Senate Kenyon Committee, he admitted a net worth of $350,000, although his annual salary as sheriff was only $3,500, and his previous salary as county clerk was even less.

Late in 1919, Governor Cornwell appointed a commission

to investigate conditions in Logan County coal fields.[4] It reported that in 1919 the "treasurer of the Logan County Coal Operators Association paid the Logan Sheriff the sum of $32,000, and in 1920, the sum of $46,630, for salaries of deputy sheriffs." The secretary of the Association testified in Blizzard's treason trial that these amounts were correct, and added that in the first nine months of 1921, such payments rose to $61,517. No figures are available for later years.

In its report, the U. S. Senate Kenyon Committee thus condemned the Logan County deputy sheriff system:

"The system of paying deputy sheriffs out of funds contributed by the operators, as the testimony shows has been done in Logan County... is a vicious and un-American policy. Public officers should be paid out of the public treasury. It is freely admitted that the purpose of the plan is to prevent men from coming into the county to organize the United Mine Workers. Men have been driven out of the county who attempted to do so .... It would be just as logical to have members of Congress paid by certain interests, or to have judges paid by other interests."[5]

During his reign, Chafin was continuously "breathing out threatenings and slaughter" against the miners' union and frequently taunted its leaders on their inability to organize, or even enter, his county. One evening in early September, 1919, he boldly swaggered into union headquarters in the City of Charleston, and was shot and seriously wounded by Bill Petry, vice-president of the union.

Chafin's explanation of this visit was that he and a Kanawha County deputy sheriff were looking for a union employee for whom he held a warrant, issued in Logan County. But, even if true, his jurisdiction as sheriff did not extend beyond the borders of his own county. He had no authority to make arrests in Kanawha County. However, a number of persons in the union offices at the time of the shooting said

[4] See Appendix I, Note 10.
[5] See Appendix I, Note 10.

that "Chafin entered alone, was drunk, armed, and very belligerent."

A few days after the shooting, Gordon Blizzard, a union organizer, told me that he took Chafin's gun from him after he was shot, and helped him to a chair; that all of his much vaunted courage oozed out of him along with his blood, and "in whimpering tones he said: 'You have shot me; now give me a chance. Take me to a hospital.'"

Dan Cunningham, a Charleston policeman, told me that he was the first officer to enter the union offices after the shooting and he saw no Kanawha County deputy sheriff; that after his arrest, Petry threw his 22-caliber pistol into a desk drawer, and casually remarked:

"That's what happens when a man carries a toy pistol. That goddamned son-of-a-bitch is liable to get well. I should have had my old 'forty-four.'"

Chafin recovered. Petry was indicted in Kanawha County for shooting him, but the evidence so strongly supported his claim of self-defense that he was never tried.

Chapter 13

THE ARMED MARCH[1]

In late August, 1919, while Chafin was recovering from his wound, the miners in the Kanawha River and New River fields decided to carry their union into Logan County by force. Accordingly, on September 1 an army, later estimated to number 5,000 armed miners, began to assemble at the head of Lens Creek, 12 miles from Charleston, for the invasion of Chafin's stronghold.

At nine o'clock on the night of September 4, Governor John J. Cornwell visited the camp and told the mob that their undertaking was ill-advised, unthinkable, would not be tolerated, and advised the men to return to their homes. "If you have complaints of injustice," said he, "file them with me. I will investigate them, and if they are true and legitimate, I will do what I can to correct such conditions." But the mob ignored his advice and two days later began its march toward Logan County.

At the town of Danville, however, twenty miles from their starting point, the marchers read in the newspapers that the Governor had asked the President for Federal troops to "disperse the rioters," and that the leaders would be arrested and tried for treason. Alarmed, the marchers abandoned the undertaking, and special trains brought them down Coal River to Charleston, where they disbanded.

Union officers filed their grievances[2] with the Governor;

---

[1] The most complete and accurate newspaper account of the events referred to in this Chapter 13, and subsequent chapters in Part Four, are to be found in the Charleston papers, *Gazette* and *Mail*, beginning with September 1, 1919.

[2] Those grievances, as listed in the Governor's letter to Major Davis, were: "The coal operators in the Guyan (Logan) field are employing armed guards; that said guards have been beating, slugging, and maltreating workers and other persons in said field; that men are kept in the mines by threats and intimidation; that their rates of pay are below that in mines in union fields, and their living conditions infinitely worse; that a large majority of the workers in the field desire to join the Union but are forcibly prevented from doing so."

See Appendix I, Note 10.

and on September 16 he named Major Tom B. Davis, Acting Adjutant General, and Col. George S. Wallace, an able lawyer of Huntington, as a committee to investigate those complaints. The committee's work was thorough, and the voluminous evidence taken describes a dismal picture in our American industrial life. But the State's coal-controlled Legislature did nothing, and the intolerable conditions continued.

Leaders of the union during the armed march-From left to right: "General" Bill Blizzard, president of Sub-District No. 2, and commander of the "troops" in the field; Fred Mooney, secretary-treasurer; Bill Petry, vice-president (the man who shot Don Chafin); and Frank Keeney, president, District 17 of the miners' union.

But this abortive march of 1919 was only the prelude to the major rebellion in the summer of 1921. In the meantime, in Bloody Mingo County a bitter strike had been in progress for more than a year, the Matewan Massacre had taken place, the Battle of the Tug had been fought; many persons had been killed; the disturbed district was under martial law; and more than one hundred strikers and union organizers languished in the county jail.

To release the Mingo County prisoners, to crush Chafin's power in Logan County, and to unionize the miners in both counties, the union leaders in the Kanawha River and New River valleys again decided to send an army of armed miners into those two counties. In furtherance of this plan Frank Keeney, President of District 17, called on all union miners in the valley to meet on the State Capitol grounds Sunday afternoon, August 7, 1921.[3]

Shortly before the appointed hour, I left my hotel by a side door and joined the miners moving toward the Capitol. A local newspaper estimated the crowd at 5,000. Keeney introduced Old Mother Jones, and for nearly an hour that foul-mouthed, vulgar, profane, old agitator harangued the mob. She assailed Governor E. F. Morgan as a "tool of the goddamned coal operators," and inflamed the miners with stories of atrocities inflicted by mine guards upon workers in Logan and Mingo counties, most of which were pure fabrications.

President Frank Keeney then told the crowd that he had urged Governor Morgan to lift martial law in Mingo County and he had refused. "Therefore," he shouted, "you have no recourse, except to fight. The only way you can get your rights is with a high-power rifle, and the man who does not have this equipment is not a good union man." He directed the miners to return to their homes and "get ready," and await the call to mobilize.

One week later the call went out for the miners to "procure arms by any means" and assemble at the old rendezvous on Lens Creek, near Marmet, beginning August 20. In the meantime, when Mother Jones learned that the leaders of the movement would be arrested and charged with treason, she became alarmed and urged the miners to abandon the undertaking. She read a telegram to the group, which she said was sent to her by the President, ordering the miners to give up

[3] See Charleston newspapers, *Gazette* and *Mail*, of August 8, 1921.

the unlawful enterprise or Federal troops would be sent to crush the insurrection.

Some of the mob leaders thought the telegram was spurious. Keeney told Mother that the men doubted the genuineness of the message and asked to see it. She told him to "go straight to hell," and returned to Charleston. An inquiry sent to the White House by Keeney brought the reply that no message had been sent to Mother Jones. That incident ended Mother's influence among the miners, and she left the State—never to return.[4]

At the time there was much talk among the miners that Mother Jones had "sold out to the operators." But, in the summer of 1962, Frank Keeney said to me: "No, Mother Jones never took money from the operators. At that time she was 91 years old, and age had quenched much of the fighting spirit that characterized her earlier years."

Despite the defection of Mother Jones, preparations for the march continued. The union counties had been thoroughly combed for guns and ammunition, and by August 24 mobilization was complete, with about 6,000 well armed and adequately provisioned miners present. "Old Peg-Leg" Lawrence Dwyer, of Beckley, member of the International Executive Board of the miners' union, secretly delivered to the group the old machine gun and 3,000 rounds of ammunition stolen by strikers from the Baldwin-Felts mine guards at Willis Branch the year before.[5]

On the evening of August 24, 1921, the army moved out of Lens Creek camp and began the 65-mile march to Logan Town, its first objective. The avowed purposes of the marchers, as testified by some of the participants, were to hang Don Chafin in the courthouse yard in Logan; overthrow martial law in Mingo County and liberate all strikers and union organizers held in jail; and unionize all miners in both Logan and Mingo counties.

---

[4] These facts were given to me in the summer of 1962 by Frank Keeney. See also Appendix I, Note 5.
[5] See Appendix II, "Destruction of Willis Branch."

The Governor asked the President for Federal troops to suppress the revolt. The President issued a proclamation warning the miners to desist from their unlawful purpose and sent General H. H. Bandholtz to the scene to urge compliance with his order. The Governor and the General called Keeney to the Governor's office and warned him that the undertaking was armed rebellion against the State, and unless the miners disbanded and returned to their homes at once, they would be dispersed by Federal troops and the union leaders charged with treason against the State.

The following day the General and Kenney went to the camp of the marchers and induced them to abandon the enterprise and return to their homes. Satisfied that the trouble was over, the General departed that night for Washington.

"But," said the miners, "Chafin did not want peace." The night Bandholtz left, he sent a strong detachment of his mine guards, accompanied by a few State Police, across Blair Mountain into union territory to arrest certain marchers for whom warrants had been issued in Logan County.

Without reason, said the marchers, the officers fired on them, killed two of their number, wounded three, and then retreated back into Logan County. But Capt. J. R. Brockus, who commanded this detachment of State Police, reported that the marchers attacked the officers first, and that the latter fired only in self-defense.

Reports of this incident, greatly magnified no doubt, spread rapidly through the mountains and the following morning the miners resumed their march.

The "Commander" of this army was the late "General" Bill Blizzard, youthful union leader scarcely out of his teens, President of Sub-District No. 2, which embraced Paint Creek and Cabin Creek. Hundreds of his "troops" were former soldiers of World War I, and the entire enterprise was conducted with strict military precision. All highways were thoroughly patrolled by armed miners. Passwords were required in order to move about the countryside. The first password was "To Mingo." To enable them to distinguish friend from foe, the marchers tied red handkerchiefs around their necks, and were called "Red Necks." The defenders identified themselves by white arm bands, and were called "Whites."

The miners drafted three doctors and a half-dozen nurses, and forced them to join in the enterprise to care for their sick and wounded. Railroad trains were commandeered for the transportation of men and supplies, and stores along the line of march were broken into and robbed of all food, guns, and ammunition.

With such speed did "General" Blizzard move his troops that in less than 36 hours after the alleged attack by Logan mine guards and State Police, his entire army had concentrated at the headwaters of Little Coal River, ready for the march across rugged Blair Mountain into Chafin's stronghold of Logan County.

In the meantime, Chafin was busy recruiting an army to repel the invasion. He even opened the jail to all inmates who would volunteer to fight. But all prisoners would not fight for Chafin. Floyd Greggs filed his affidavit with the U. S. Senate Kenyon Committee in which he stated, in substance, that he arrived in Logan August 24, looking for work; that he was arrested immediately and lodged in jail; that five days later two deputies took him to Chafin's office, and Chafin asked him if he had been in the army; that he said, "Yes, in the marines"; that Chafin ordered him to select a rifle and join the forces moving to the front, and he refused; that Chafin put the muzzle of a pistol in his face and said, "You will either fight or die"; that he still refused, and Chafin ordered him returned to his cell.

On September 1, continued Greggs in his affidavit, he saw a union bricklayer from Huntington shot to death in the jail corridor, not three feet from his cell, because he refused to fight. Two shots were fired by the deputy. Two deputies then took the dead man by the feet and dragged the body from the jail, across the railroad tracks toward the river. Greggs also stated that he was released at midnight, September 3, and told by a deputy to be out of the county by daylight, or "have your goddamned brains blown out."

Clomar Stanfield, another jail inmate who refused to fight,

filed a similar affidavit with the Senate Committee, in which he also told of seeing the Huntington bricklayer murdered in the jail by a deputy sheriff.

Chafin sent out a distress call to other nonunion coal counties, urging them to send immediate assistance. Hundreds of former soldiers, eager for new adventures, and scores of Baldwin-Felts mine guards and deputy sheriffs responded, until he had an army of 3,000 men, all better armed than the miners, and supported by 150 State Police armed with machine guns, sub-machine guns, and tear gas bombs.

The defenders were the first to reach the summit of bleak, rugged, Blair Mountain chain. They deployed along the crest for a distance of fifteen miles, hastily threw up breastworks, and waited for the attack.

In the early morning of September 1, a large force of miners advanced up White's Trace Branch to attack the defenders on Blair Mountain. On the way, they fought a skirmish with a small outpost of mine guards, and John Gore, A. C. Cafalgo, and George Munsey, all Logan deputies, and one attacking miner were killed. The miners captured a number of prisoners, including a son of Deputy Gore. Later, these prisoners told gruesome stories of how they were beaten to force them to disclose the number of defenders on Blair Mountain. Young Gore was taunted about the death of his father and frequently threatened with the same fate. But all prisoners were released after the arrival of Federal troops.

For two days there was intermittent sniping between the advanced posts. A few commercial airplane pilots, employed by the operators, attempted to drop explosive bombs on the camps of the marchers. But they missed their targets, and the bombs exploded harmlessly on the mountainside.

At daylight, on the morning of September 3, 3,000 invaders advanced in the first general assault. The fighting soon became active along the entire front. At intervals and from different positions along the battle line was heard the rat-tat-tat of the old machine gun from Willis Branch. But, after three hours, the marchers retired, bearing their dead and wounded with them. Shortly after noon the attack was renewed along the entire front; and for four hours the battle raged; but, again, the attackers failed to reach the top of the mountain barrier.

Those were not sham battles. The men who contended on that steep mountainside were filled with deadly hate, and they fought to kill. Dr. Miliken, a company doctor at Blair mining camp, testified in Walter Allen's treason trial that the firing "was sharp at times. I was in the Spanish-American War, and I heard about as much shooting on Blair Mountain as I heard in Manila."[6]

In the meantime, the Governor again had asked the President for immediate military aid in suppressing the insurrection. While the fighting was fiercest, General Bandholtz arrived with 2,000 Federal troops. At Barboursville he divided his forces. He sent 1,000 men under the command of Major Smart up Coal River, to the rear of the attacking miners, while he advanced with the remaining 1,000 troops up the Guyandotte River, to the rear of the defenders. The two commands arrived at the battle front at four o'clock in the afternoon of September 3 and ordered both sides to cease hostilities. The order was obeyed. Most of the miners were disarmed, but many hid their guns and ammunition in the mountains and went back for them later.

Neither side made any announcement of their casualties, either in dead or wounded. But after he returned to Bluefield, Hughey Lucas, a Baldwin-Felts mine guard, told me that he counted ten dead "Red Necks" in his sector.

At least one national officer of the miners' union shared in responsibility for the uprising. Vice-President Philip Murray, later head of the C.I.O., secretly visited the battle front and gave encouragement to the criminal undertaking. In his testimony before the Kenyon Senate Committee, he admitted that in his report to the national convention of the union, he had said:

"I visited the battle front, met with large numbers of the citizens' army, discussed every phase of the so-called insurrec-

---

[6] From Record of Walter Allen's Treason Trial, page 604.

ton with them, and am satisfied in my own mind that if Federal troops had not arrived in the State of West Virginia at the time they did, there would have been very little cause of further complaint from anyone about further activities of the Baldwin-Felts mine guards in the State of West Virginia, as it was self-evident to any casual observer that the outcome was inevitable, as the citizens' army was making steady advance into the camp of the enemy."[7]

But that was a "pep talk" to convention delegates. The cold facts are that the marchers never even reached nonunion territory. The winding crest of Blair Mountain was the dividing line between the union field of Coal River Valley and the nonunion territory of the Guyandotte River Valley (Logan County). After nine hours of fighting, the attacking miners failed to reach the mountain top at any point.

While the attackers outnumbered the defenders, probably two to one, the latter were better armed and supported by 150 State Police armed with machine guns, sub-machine guns, and tear gas bombs, as against one obsolete machine gun in the hands of the mob. Moreover, the defenders were fighting from previously prepared trenches and other defensive positions, and were being reinforced hourly. A continuation of the battle for any considerable length of time would have resulted in staggering casualties among the miners, as well as their certain failure to dislodge the defenders from the crest of Blair Mountain.

Who was to blame for this bloody blot on the State's history? A staff correspondent for the Washington Star, in a dispatch sent to his paper from the battle front on September 2, 1921, said:

> Everywhere one goes down in this country he hears the name of Don Chafin, high sheriff of Logan County. One can see that he has struck terror in the hearts of the people of the union fields. Although a state officer, they do not trust him. Every kind of crime is charged to him and his dep-

---

[7] See Report of Kenyon Senate Committee, page 671.

uties. He is king of the "Kingdom of Logan." He reigns supreme by virtue of a state machine, backed by the power of the operators. It is Don Chafin upon whom the miners and the people of this section place the blame for this latest blot in the State's history.

Chapter 14

TREASON

The scene now shifted from the battlefield to the courtroom. The Logan County boundary line is a few miles east of Blair Mountain, and the battle was fought and the killings occurred in Logan County. Immediately, its circuit judge convened a special grand jury to indict the marchers.

C. W. Osenton and A. M. Beicher, two highly paid lawyers for the coal operators, known among the miners as the "Coal Dust Twins," were appointed assistant prosecuting attorneys of the county. They prepared, and the grand jury voted, indictments charging Frank Keeney, Fred Mooney, Bill Petry, and Bill Blizzard, union leaders, and 525 marchers, with murder, conspiracy to commit murder, accessory to murder, and treason against the State of West Virginia. The regular grand jury, that convened a month later, charged 210 additional marchers with the same crimes.

For many years Beicher had been the attorney for the miners' union, and was one of the union lawyers in the military-court trials during the martial law periods on Paint Creek and Cabin Creek.[1] But the union leaders said that the coal operators acquired his talents and the future plans of the union by offering him more money than the union could pay.[2]

That many of these indictments were justified cannot be gainsaid. The enterprise was levying war against the State of West Virginia and its constituted authorities, and hence was treason within the constitutional meaning of that term. Therefore, the union leaders who instigated the uprising, and all those who took part in it, were guilty of treason. And, inasmuch as the undertaking was unlawful in its purpose and resulted in numerous killings, they were also guilty of murder.

[1] See Chapter 4.
[2] In the trials at Charles Town, the defense was also assisted by C. J. Van Fleet, a union attorney from Pittsburgh, and James M. Mason, Jr., a local lawyer.

Yet it is doubtful if a dozen participants in the march understood that they were fighting the sovereign State; and all would have resented the imputation that they were guilty of treason. In their minds, they were fighting the hated mine guards, and for their constitutional and statutory rights.

Immediately, the roundup of prisoners began. Hundreds were arrested in Kanawha, Boone, Raleigh, and Fayette counties, and taken to Logan County, where every effort was made to extort confessions from them and induce them to testify against the union leaders. The Logan jail was soon filled, neighboring counties refused to receive any of the prisoners, and hundreds had to be turned loose on their promise to appear in court when notified. But about seventy-five of the more active participants in the uprising were denied bond and held in the Logan County jail to await trial.

In the meantime Keeney and Mooney had been indicted in Mingo County as accessories to murder, and were held in jail in that county. About that time, however, the union employed Tom Townsend, a very competent and astute Charleston lawyer, to assist its regular attorney, Harold Houston, in defending the marchers.

Townsend was one of the political bosses of Kanawha County, and he quickly enlisted the help of the county authorities in his efforts to keep the union leaders out of the hands of Sheriff Chafin. Immediately, a special grand jury was assembled and indictments were returned by it charging Keeney, Mooney, Petry, and Blizzard with certain alleged offenses committed in the county at the beginning of the march. Shortly thereafter Keeney and Mooney were released on bond in Mingo County. They were quickly taken into custody by Kanawha County deputy sheriffs, brought to Charleston, and lodged in the county jail. Legally, they were then prisoners of Kanawha County and it did not have to surrender them to Chafin. They were special prisoners, however, and came and went as they pleased.

But the union quartet decided that, if they remained free, while the rank and file of the miners languished in jail they would "lose face" with the workers, and also jeopardize their positions as union officers. They telephoned Sheriff Chafin that they were ready to surrender and place themselves under his personal protection. To effectuate the surrender, they asked Chafin to meet them in Huntington. The surrender was arranged, and the prisoners were taken to the Logan County jail.

Later, Keeney told me that as they walked from the depot to the jail a woman on the sidewalk said to her companion: "There goes that damn Frank Keeney. I sure would like to put a bullet in his back." For 59 days the prisoners were kept on the crowded top floor of the county jail, and "every day," said Keeney later, "we expected to get bullets in our backs."

Meantime, while the union leaders were in jail, Harold Houston, a Charleston lawyer, counsel for the miners' union, began a nationwide campaign among union workers to raise money for the "Miners Defense Funds." He soon had a "War Chest" of over fifty thousand dollars.

Lawyer Townsend told me that as soon as he was assured of "safe conduct" by Chafin, he went to Logan to confer with his many clients held in jail. On the jail "blotter" were numerous names with only the letters "R. N." written after each one. Turning to the keeper of the "bastille," he said:

"What is the meaning of the letters 'R. N.' after these names?"

"'Red Neck,' by God!" answered the jailer.

"But that is no violation of the law," suggested the attorney.

"By God, Don [meaning Chafin] says it's a felony, and he's the law over here," responded the jail keeper.

Finally, one morning before daylight, a deputy jailer came to the cell door and said: "Keeney, get up. The Boss wants you downstairs." As he dressed, Keeney said to Mooney and Blizzard, "Boys, I think this is it. If I don't come back, keep your mouths shut until you get out, and then tell the world." Chafin took Keeney to a nearby restaurant for breakfast, and then they boarded a train for Huntington. On the train, Chafin said to his prisoner: "We are sending all miners' cases to another county for trial. The lawyers are meeting in Huntington today to decide on the county, and I thought you should be present."

Jefferson County, in the extreme eastern part of the State, was agreed upon; and the next day the three union leaders were released on bond.[3]

Charles Town, governmental seat of staid old Jefferson County, is 250 miles by railroad from Logan Town. In 1859, in its ancient and historical courthouse, "Old John Brown of Osawatomie" had been convicted of treason against the Commonwealth of Virginia for his attack on Harpers Ferry Arsenal and hanged just outside the village.

The county is wholly agricultural, and, to influence prospective farmer-jurors, both sides began to spread the wildest propaganda throughout the county. Voting lists were copied and the county flooded with the most lurid and inflammatory literature. Also, the union sent spurious book agents and sewing machine salesmen into the county to make personal contact with farm families, and "incidentally" remark that they had just worked Logan County, and had seen "first hand" how brutally the "coal barons and their mine guards abused and oppressed the miners." Of course, those glib gentlemen were highly paid propagandists who had never even seen Logan County. The people soon took sides, and the quiet community divided into two violently hostile camps—pro-union and anti-union.

The trials were scheduled to begin April 24, 1922, and three days before a special train called the "Red Special," with Frank Keeney as generalissimo and carrying defense attorneys and 1,000 defendants and witnesses, left Charleston for the trial city. The same day a special day coach loaded with prisoners, guarded by Chafin's deputies, was started from Logan for the same destination. The following day, lawyers for the prosecution, witnesses for the State, coal operators, private court reporters, and newsmen, also left Charleston by special train for Charles Town.[4]

---

[3] These details were told to me by Frank Keeney, personally, during the summer of 1962.

[4] See Charleston newspapers, *Gazette* and *Mail*, of August 21, 1922, and subsequent issues.

The little town was crowded to capacity. The prisoners were lodged in jail; the union established temporary quarters for billeting and feeding its 1,000 defendants and witnesses; and the lawyers, coal operators, court reporters, newsmen, and State Police, took over the small hotels and rooming houses. Meanwhile, the townspeople complained bitterly because of "all this trash dumped in on us."

Feeling between the opposing sides ran high, but 40 heavily armed State Police patrolled the streets and kept peace between the factions.

Trial day arrived. Court convened with the very able John Marshall Woods as presiding judge. The Logan County Prosecuting Attorney surrendered the prosecution to the "Coal Dust Twins"—Osenton and Belcher—while Tom Townsend and Harold Houston carried the burden for the defense. Osenton was from Fayette County, and Townsend had practiced law there a few years before coming to Charleston. They hated each other intensely. Townsend had a low, well-modulated voice, while Osenton was loud and boisterous. They soon clashed, and Osenton began shouting. The Judge rapped his gavel for silence, and then quietly observed:

"Gentlemen, the Court's sense of hearing is very acute. I have not been told, nor have I observed, that any one of the very able counsel in the case is troubled with defective hearing. Therefore, hereafter, let your oral observations be couched in more natural and softer tones."

This reprimand took away much of Osenton's steam.

Defense counsel demanded separate trials for their clients—a right guaranteed to them by law. Counsel for the State argued that such a course would convert the proceedings into a comedy, as it would take fifty years to try all the defendants separately. During the discussion, a tall, lank mountaineer arose in the rear of the court room and gravely addressed the Court:

"Your Honor," he said, "may I say a word?"

Being advised by counsel that they did not recognize the inquirer, the Court said:

"You are a citizen, and have a right to be heard. What is it, sir?"

"Your Honor," said the mountaineer, "I'm one of the defendants. Both sides agree that it will take fifty years to try all these cases; and, if it's all the same to you, Sir, I'd like to have my case tried last.'"

Separate trials were ordered. Five weeks were spent in the trial of General Bill Blizzard, charged with treason. The State proved by scores of witnesses that he was one of the main instigators of the march; that he was present with, and in

Left—"General" Bill Blizzard at the time of his trial in Charles Town. Right—Courthouse in Charles Town where "Old John Brown" and "General" Bill Blizzard were tried for treason.

[5] This story was told to me by both Harold Houston and Tom Townsend, defense attorneys.

actual command of, the marchers at all times—giving commands and issuing orders. Many of the witnesses against him were miners—former members of his army.

Blizzard's defense was an alibi—that he had no part in organizing the march; that he neither aided nor abetted the undertaking; that he made only one contact with the marchers, and that was to try to persuade them to abandon the enterprise; and, with that exception, he was in the union offices in Charleston during the entire time the march was in progress. He was supported by a cloud of witnesses, mostly co-defendants.

Blizzard was acquitted, and the verdict was the signal for a wild demonstration. He was carried to the street on the shoulders of young miners—ex-servicemen. A parade was started, miners and a few townspeople joined the procession to honor the smiling youth whose courage they admired, and who symbolized for them the side of the struggle with which they sympathized, but which they did not fully comprehend.

Blizzard's acquittal greatly alarmed the operators. They immediately employed a number of persons, including a few country preachers, to spread anti-union propaganda throughout the county. These hirelings painted the miners' union as an ogreish institution, headed by criminals, that was responsible for the high prices the public was then paying for coal. Of course, this poison campaign bore its expected fruit—widespread prejudice against all the defendants.

I was in Washington and decided to return by way of Charles Town and look in upon these trials. On trial at the time were Rev. J. W. Wilburn, a miner and mountain Baptist preacher, and his son John, charged jointly with the murder of John Gore, a notorious Logan mine guard, killed in the skirmish between outposts just before the main "Battle of Blair Mountain."

The elder Wilburn was a stolid mountaineer, a powerfully framed man, but battered and stooped from toil, with a hard and tragic look in his eyes. He joined the marchers with the ringing declaration: "it is time to lay aside the Bible and take up my rifle." But in the prisoner's dock he was a pathetic figure. His voice was low, and his movements so slow and unhurried that he seemed a part of his native mountains. He had little education and could not comprehend the drama in which he was the chief actor; and "like father, like son." Like so many others, they were mere chips tossed aimlessly hither and yon by the eddies and crosscurrents of that bitter industrial conflict. Both were convicted of murder in the second degree and sentenced to eleven years in the penitentiary. Both were paroled by Governor Howard M. Gore in 1925.

Hundreds of miners from Raleigh County, 75 miles from Logan Town, had joined in the march. They were led by young Walter Allen, head of the Dry Branch local union, who was next tried and convicted of treason, and sentenced to ten years in the penitentiary. However, while his appeal was pending in the Supreme Court, he disappeared and never has been found. The union paid the State his forfeited bond of $10,000.

Thus far, all those tried were actual participants in the march. But Frank Keeney, president of District 17 of the miners' union and the behind-the-scenes director of the undertaking, was the next defendant called for trial, on a charge of treason. But, by that time, the public mind had been so poisoned that even the presiding Judge stated from the bench that the prisoner could not get a fair trial in the county, and his case was transferred to the adjoining county of Morgan. There, public sentiment so strongly favored the defendant that the indictment against him was dismissed by counsel for the operators.

All remaining cases were then transferred to Greenbrier County, another quiet agricultural community.

Chapter 15

THE GREENBRIER FIASCO[1]

As soon as it was announced that future trials had been transferred to Greenbrier County, union agents hurried to Lewisburg, aristocratic county-seat town, and engaged every room in an old hotel near the courthouse. An old phonograph was procured and a call went out to local unions to collect from the mountain folk a number of records of religious hymns, and bring them to Lewisburg.

General Bill Blizzard was the first defendant to go on trial, June 18, 1923, upon an indictment charging him with being an accessory to the murder of George Muncy, a Logan County mine guard, killed in the skirmish between outposts just before the "Battle of Blair Mountain."

The day before the trial began, the old phonograph was set up on the hotel porch, and every morning for a half hour before the opening of court, and each evening after it adjourned, the jurors were regaled with old-time, soul-stirring hymns, intended to arouse in them a deep sense of religious fervor. Frequently, a quartet or larger group of miners and their wives would join in the singing. Occasionally, after a "song service," a mountain miner preacher would pray loudly and eloquently for the Lord "to open the eyes of the blind and unstop the ears of the deef, and see that jestice is done."

But this simulated religious fervor was only well-planned propaganda, intended to convince the country jurors that the miners were a law-abiding, God-fearing people—victims of a relentless persecution.

After a trial that lasted five weeks, the jury failed to agree on a verdict. But throughout the trial, the prosecution was under two insurmountable handicaps—two of the State's most important witnesses had been murdered, and one juror

[1] This chapter is based entirely upon reports in the Charleston newspapers, *Gazette* and *Mail*, court records of Greenbrier and Fayette counties, West Virginia Supreme Court, and the Circuit Court of Meigs County, Ohio.

had been bribed by a union agent to hold out for a verdict of "not guilty."

Two days before Blizzard's trial opened, Ed Reynolds and J. W. Swanner were brutally murdered in Rutland, Meigs County, Ohio, by J. R. Miller, one of the indicted marchers who had escaped from West Virginia. These witnesses had worked closely with the union leaders during the uprising. After being promised immunity, they had testified for the State in all previous trials. In substance, Reynolds' evidence was that Blizzard was the actual leader at the "front" throughout the march and that he had led one of Blizzard's divisions and received his orders directly from Blizzard at all times. He was corroborated by Swanner.

The union leaders decreed that these two "traitors to the cause of labor" must die before Blizzard's trial in Greenbrier County. In furtherance of this plan, Miller wrote Reynolds from his Ohio hideout that he would testify for the prosecution, if given immunity, and asked Reynolds to make the arrangements. Reynolds made the deal, and he and Swanner went to Rutland, Ohio, to bring Miller to the trials at Lewisburg. But Savoy Holt, a rabid union organizer who had been keeping watch, left Charleston just ahead of them. He arrived first at Miller's home and told him of the approach of the messengers.

Miller lay in wait in his home for his unsuspecting and unarmed victims. As they stepped upon his porch, he opened fire. Swanner was killed instantly. Reynolds tried to escape, but was shot three times in the back and killed before he reached the front gate. Further weighting the balance in favor of the union was the fact that a radical union agitator named G. C. Hickey had bribed H. R. Harrah, one of the jurors, to hold out for a verdict of "not guilty."

The Meigs County, Ohio, court records show that Miller was convicted of manslaughter for these killings and sentenced to the Ohio penitentiary for a term of from two to twenty years. Holt was not indicted.

Harrah and Hickey were both indicted in Greenbrier County—the former for accepting, and the latter for giving a bribe.

Harrah was convicted, but the Supreme Court set aside the conviction because of a defective indictment.[2] He was not reindicted, and the indictment against Hickey was dismissed without trial.

The State was preparing to put Blizzard on trial a second time on the same indictment when the bribery scandal broke. All remaining cases were then transferred to Fayette County, where every circumstance favored the defendants. At that time, Fayette was one of the State's largest coal-producing counties. Hundreds of its miners had participated in the march, scores were under indictment and awaiting trial, and its population was in sympathy with the marchers. Why Fayette County was selected has never been explained.

In Fayette County, Frank Keeney, president of District 17 of the miners' union, one of the chief instigators of the march, was tried and acquitted of the charge of accessory to murder. Hopelessly discouraged, the operators then directed their attorneys to dismiss all remaining indictments. This ended the abortive attempt of the coal operators to convict an army of protesting workers.

Those legal battles had extended over a period of two years and cost the State's general taxpayers over one million dollars in court costs alone.

In the winter of 1942-43 I was a neighbor of the late Harold Houston in Lake Worth, Florida. In one of our many conversations, I said:

"Mr. Houston, you were chief counsel for the miners during the 'treason trials.' After the lapse of twenty years, what is your opinion as to whether Bill Blizzard was the actual leader and in command of the miners in that march?"

"Blizzard," said he, "was the only man among the union leaders capable of organizing and leading such an undertaking. And it is my present opinion that he was the organizer of the enterprise, and its actual commander and leader in the field."

"Then," I said, "the cloud of witnesses who testified in the

[2] See *State vs. Harrah*, 101 West Virginia Supreme Court Reports, page 300.

trial that Blizzard was in the union offices in Charleston during the entire time of the march were perjurers?"

"Undoubtedly, that is true," he replied.

However, the Armed March was a tragic disaster for the miners' union. It bankrupted its local treasuries, caused the miners to lose confidence in its officers, alienated all public sympathy, and strengthened the contention of the operators that it was a lawless organization.

At the time of the Armed March, John L. Lewis had been president of the miners' union less than a year. The local union leaders unwisely entered upon the uprising without consulting him, and he was bitterly resentful of their actions in, as he said, "trying to shoot the union into West Virginia." He aided in their defense, however, and made a couple of visits to the trials in Charles Town. But when the trials were all over he summarily dismissed Petty, Keeney, Mooney, and Blizzard[3] from their union posts, and fired Harold Houston as union counsel.

Lewis appointed Percy Tetlow as acting-president of District 17 of the miners' union, but there was nothing for him to take over. By that time Yellow-Dog Contracts and injunctions excluded the union from West Virginia's southern mountains.

---

[3] In 1933, when the miners were unionized nationally, T. C. Townsend was made general counsel for the union, and he persuaded Lewis to name Blizzard as president of the union's District 17, with headquarters in Charleston.

Chapter 16

THE PASSING OF THE CZAR

With the failure of the Armed March, Chafin became more arrogant. He issued a ukase that all union sympathizers found in his county would be "dealt with summarily." This challenge was accepted by the Rev. Henry L. Huntington, editor of *Christian Work*, and Arthur Garfield Hays, attorney, both of New York City. They announced through the press that on Sunday, March 4, 1923, at 2 p. m., they would speak on "Constitutional Liberty" from the front steps of the courthouse in Logan Town.

The Czar decreed that the meeting should not be held; but the operators feared that the unfavorable publicity of such refusal might adversely affect coal sales in large eastern cities, and directed him to permit the meeting.

The speakers arrived at the appointed hour, accompanied by a half-dozen reporters. Mastin White, a prominent citizen of the town, publicly invited the visitors to speak from his front porch, should they be denied the courthouse steps. A large crowd assembled, and the meeting was held at the time and place scheduled. Valley Gould, a union employee of the railroad, acted as chairman. For two hours the speakers assailed the tyranny of the coal operators and their "political hirelings."[1] A couple of days later, Mastin White was assaulted and severely beaten by Chafin's deputy-thugs, and the chairman of the meeting was driven from the county.

With the end of the treason trials, Chafin's power began to crumble. While serving as one of his deputies, Tennis Hatfield, youngest son of old "Devil Anse," also operated a roadhouse known as the "Blue Goose." In this rude hostelry, located only a few miles up the gorge from the town of Logan, in open defiance of both Federal and State prohibition laws, the mountain Boniface dispensed "moonshine" whiskey to the thirsty miners. In due time he fell into the

---

[1] See Charleston newspapers, *Gazette* and *Mail*, of Monday, March 5, 1923.

hands of stern old Judge McClintic of the United States District Court, and was sent to jail for six months.

While in jail Hatfield disclosed that Sheriff Chafin had been his partner in the liquor business and had received one half the profits. Chafin was indicted in the Federal Court at Huntington for conspiracy to violate the national prohibition laws. The Czar was desperate, while his kinsmen and deputies breathed dire threats against the Hatfields—another mountain feud was in the making.

In the meantime, old "Devil Anse" was dead, and the leadership of the clan had passed to his oldest living son, Cap Hatfield, the most deadly killer of the feud. He counseled peace, at least until he could talk with Chafin.

On Sunday morning the grim old killer donned his steel breastplate, mounted his mule, and with a 45-caliber pistol conveniently holstered under his arm and his faithful Winchester resting carelessly on the pommel of his saddle, rode down the canyon to Logan Town. At Chafin's home, he threw the bridle reins over a gatepost and strode up to the porch where sat the Czar reading a newspaper account of his indictment.

"Don," said Cap, "I fetch you peace or war. Which do you want?"

"Why, Uncle Cap, what do you mean?"

"I hear that you and my brother, Tennis, are havin' some trouble. And I just want to say to you, Don, that nothin' must happen to the boy."

"Why, Uncle Cap, you know that I wouldn't hurt Tennis."

"Oh! I know you wouldn't. I ain't afeared of that. But I am afeared that one of your cut-throats will shoot him in the back; and I want you to know that if anything happens to Tennis, you will have to answer to me personally. Good Day, Don."

Having delivered his ultimatum, Cap remounted his mule and left the town as quietly as he had come, pausing at the courthouse only long enough to leave a final warning with one of Chafin's deputies.

"You know, John," he said, "I am a man of peace. I ain't killed a man for a little more than twenty years, and I've joined the Baptist Church. But I warn you fellows, nothin' better happen to Tennis."[2]

Of course, "nothin'" happened to Tennis.

On his trial day Sheriff Chafin blustered into the city of Huntington, accompanied by a number of his deputies as a bodyguard, all heavily armed and arrogant to the point of insolence. The purpose of the bodyguard was to impress the jury and intimidate witnesses against him. In the meantime, Cap Hatfield had been appointed a deputy United States marshal, and he was directed by the Court to search and disarm all persons entering the courtroom. One by one, as they reached the door, Chafin and his guards had their guns taken from them by the doughty old feudist, and the trial passed without incident.[3]

But a court and a jury that he could not control was a new experience for Chafin, and he was convicted and sentenced to two years in the penitentiary and fined $10,000. However, powerful political influences and a Presidential parole cut short his sentence by several months.

Upon his return from the penitentiary, the swashbuckling mountaineer stepped off the train in Logan Town in the midst of a great "homecoming celebration" in his honor. There was a parade, band music, and welcoming speeches by leading Democratic politicians of the city and county, to which the Czar responded, said a local paper, in "terse but fitting remarks."

Unabashed, Chafin immediately assumed his old position of leadership in the Democratic party, county and State. During the next session of the Legislature he maintained headquarters in a Charleston hotel and lobbied for the coal interests. The House of Delegates generously accorded him

[2] Cap Hatfield related this incident to the late Judge George W. McClintic during Chafin's trial, and the Judge gave the details to me.
[3] These facts were given to me by Judge McClintic, who presided at Chafin's trial.

the "privilege of the floor," and he swaggered through the aisles of the legislative chamber with a pistol holstered lightly under his arm. He frequently occupied the dais beside Speaker J. Alf Taylor, and advised with him on legislative matters.

A few Democratic legislators resented this bold attempt to "Loganize" the Legislature and the Democratic party. But only the fire-eating septuagenarian, Jack Wilkinson, Democratic member from Cabell County, dared to denounce Chafin from the floor. Pointing his finger directly at the swaggering lobbyist, he demanded that the Legislature purge itself of his baleful influence. Quivering with rage he shouted: "I'm not afraid of this Logan outlaw if he does carry a gun in every pocket."[4] But no action was taken and the incident was soon forgotten.

In the meantime, changes were taking place in Logan County. Tennis Hatfield, upon his release from jail, changed his politics to Republican. In 1924 he was the Republican candidate for sheriff against Chafin's hand-picked Democratic candidate—Emmett Scaggs. In a contested election the local court, controlled by Chafin, declared the latter elected, but the State's Supreme Court gave the office to Hatfield on the grounds that "unconscionable frauds" had been committed by Chafin and his henchmen.[5]

But conditions in the county did not improve. Knowing how his predecessor had profited from the office, Tennis conducted it in keeping with former practices. The political principles of the gunmen who served as deputies under Chafin went no deeper than their salary checks, and they changed their politics and became deputies under Hatfield. In all respects the old order continued, except the coal operators paid Hatfield instead of Chafin.

In August, 1926, Tom Townsend, attorney for the miners' union; Van A. Bittner, president of its District 17; and two representatives from its national headquarters, drove into Logan Town. They had advertised their coming by printed

[4] I was present in the House Chamber and heard Wilkinson's attack on Chafin.
[5] *Hatfield vs. Scaggs*, 101 West Virginia Supreme Court Reports, page 425.

handbills dropped into mining camps from airplanes. At the edge of town they were surrounded by a reception committee of about twenty heavily armed mine guards, who escorted them to a hotel, without giving them a chance to speak to even one of the hundreds of miners who loitered along the streets.

In a few minutes, a committee from the local chamber of commerce visited them and demanded that they leave the county immediately. Sheriff Tennis Hatfield also called and ordered them to leave at once or he would not be responsible for their personal safety. But the union leaders remained until the next morning, always under the watchful eyes of the mine guards, when they left for Mingo County, followed by a score of guards.[6]

In the meantime, on January 1, 1929, Joe Hatfield succeeded his brother Tennis as Sheriff of Logan County, and he conducted the office in keeping with former practices.

In the summer of 1935, after the enactment by Congress of the National Labor Relations Act, commonly known as the NRA, Van Bittner returned to Logan County to organize the miners. An estimated 5,000 workers attended his first meeting; and, as he was administering the union oath of allegiance to that vast throng, he glanced around and saw former sheriff Tennis Hatfield standing beside him with uplifted right hand, swearing to support the Constitution of the United Mine Workers of America. Bittner stopped the proceedings long enough to tell Tennis that this was a "meeting of miners," not a "convention of mine guards," and if he wanted to join the union he would first have to get a job in a coal mine.[7] Tennis was never received into the fellowship of the miners union.

But what of Chafin? Repudiated by the Democratic party in his native county, openly shunned by its State leaders because of his unpopularity with the workers, stripped of all

---

[6] These facts were given to me by both Townsend and Bittner.
[7] This incident was told to me by Van Bittner shortly after his first union organizational meeting of Logan County miners.

civil authority, deserted by his old gang, this erstwhile Don Juan of the mountains left Logan County in 1934. He acquired the ten-story Guaranty Bank Building in the city of Huntington, West Virginia, for $400,000, built the city's only penthouse on its top, where he lived in semi-retirement until his death on August 9, 1954. He is said to have left an estate of more than one million dollars.

Chapter 17

SLOT MACHINES AND MURDER[1]

The State Supreme Court in *Hatfield vs. Scaggs, supra,* ended the rule of the Czar. The shooting war of the Armed March was over. But the conditions in Logan County that brought about the uprising remained untouched.

One afternoon in early January, 1931, Governor William G. Conley asked me to join him and Naaman Jackson, Judge of the Circuit Court of Logan County, in the Governor's office, to discuss conditions in that county.

"Since Don Chafin began his reign in Logan County in 1913," began the Judge, "the county has had a tradition of lawlessness, and much of that criminal activity has been traceable directly to the Sheriff's office. That is the situation today.

"Joe Hatfield is our present Sheriff, having succeeded his brother Tennis. It is freely talked in the town of Logan today that during the last campaign Joe and some other candidates borrowed a sizable sum of money for campaign purposes; and to get the money to pay this loan they have installed about two hundred slot machines in the county, probably seventy-five of them in the city of Logan. I do not know whether this rumor is true or not. But I do know that these gambling devices could not be operated in the county without the protection of the Sheriff. The machines are designed to accommodate all classes of gamblers-dime, quarter, half dollar, and dollar. A few are in the vicinity of school buildings, and some children gamble away their lunch money.

"The Logan City Council is opposed to these machines being operated in the city, and a few weeks ago it ordered the chief of police, Lon Browning, to arrest all persons who have such gambling devices on their premises. The Chief promptly resigned, with the remark: 'Gentlemen, I am not ready to die.'

[1] See Appendix I, Note 11, for statements of Hon. Vincent Legg, Governor Conley's Executive Assistant, and Mr. Frank Gibson, State policeman.

"A few days later the Council named Roy Knotts as the new chief, and gave him a number of warrants for the arrest of the owners of business places where the machines were being operated. For several months Knotts had been the head of the Logan detachment of the State Police, and was an outstanding young officer. When he resigned from the State Police, he had to turn in his state-owned service pistol; and the morning after his appointment he went to a hardware store and ordered a pistol, which had to be sent from Huntington. He next entered a cigar store and pool room, called the 'Smoke Shop,' to purchase cigarettes, and as he stood by the counter, with his back toward the door, a notorious killer named Enoch Scaggs walked up behind him, pulled a pistol and shot him five times in the back. Knotts died on the way to the hospital. The warrants for the arrest of the slot machine operators, soaked with his blood, were found in his pocket. Scaggs has been indicted and is now in jail awaiting trial.

"Another deplorable situation in the county, a hangover from Chafin days, is that this gang maintains a motley crew of lesser hoodlums who are professional perjurers, and who will swear to any falsehood to protect one of their number. In this Knotts' case the facts are exactly as I have stated, but there will be a dozen of these perjurers who will testify that they were present and saw the shooting; that Knotts assaulted Scaggs first, threw his hand back toward his hip pocket like he was reaching for a gun, and that Scaggs shot in self-defense. It is also a sad commentary that many of these lesser thugs have been commissioned special constables, with authority to carry a gun, by justices of the peace. They strut around wearing tin badges with the words 'Special Constable' on them and carrying a big gun within easy reach.

"Our prosecuting attorney is grossly incompetent, and drunk most of his waking hours. If he tried to clean up the situation, he probably would meet the same fate as Knotts. He knows this, and is afraid to try to do anything. His assistant is a cousin of the murderer of Knotts and will aid him in every way possible. The people of Logan County cannot expect any help from the prosecuting attorney's office.

"But there is still another situation in Logan County that is even more dangerous—also a hang-over from the days of Don Chafin. Under the law, the sheriff has the care and custody of trial juries in all felony cases while the trial is in progress. Of course, the sheriff does not perform this duty personally, but designates two deputies to act for him in all such cases. In Logan County these deputies, in violation of law, tell the jurors whom to convict and whom to acquit in all the more prominent cases, and the jurors are afraid either to report such conduct to the court or to decide a case contrary to the instructions of these deputies.

"In brief, gentlemen, that is the situation in Logan County. Law and order has completely broken down, and I have come to you for help."[2]

"Judge Jackson," I replied, "under our law the attorney general has no authority to go into a county to prosecute a criminal case until he is directed to do so by the governor. Therefore, the next move is up to the governor."

"Judge Jackson," said the Governor, "it appears that there is a serious situation existing in Logan County. But it is also a serious thing for the State to step in and supplant duly elected county officials. After all, conditions in Logan County are no worse today than they have been for twenty years. It is also a very serious thing for any governor to order the State's Attorney General to move into a situation where he might be killed, and this could well happen in Logan County. Personally, I would much prefer the employment of a special prosecutor in this case as did the attorney general a few years ago in the Northern coal strike. However, I shall confer further with the Attorney General tomorrow, and we will advise you of our decision."

Judge Jackson accompanied me to my office where we discussed the case in more detail. Finally, it was agreed that if

[2] Judge Jackson was not circuit judge when Don Chafin was in power. He assumed that office January 1, 1929.

I prosecuted Scaggs the Judge would call a jury from Monroe County; appoint two reputable citizens of Logan to have the care and custody of the jury during the trial; and enter an order barring both the Prosecuting Attorney and his assistant from appearing in the case in any capacity.

At my conference with the Governor the next day I asked for the assignment; and he wrote me a letter in duplicate, directing me to take over the prosecution of Enoch Scaggs in Logan County for the murder of Roy Knotts, which gave me complete and exclusive authority in the case. As he handed me the letters he said: "Remember, I am not sending you. You asked to go."

"General," the Governor continued, "you are going up against as tough a bunch of hoodlums as exist anywhere, and you, the Court, jurors, and witnesses must have adequate protection. I want you to keep a personal bodyguard with you day and night while you are in Logan County. How many State Police do you think we should have in Logan during this trial?"

"Governor," I replied, "it will be much better to have too many and not need them, than to have too few and desperately need more. There are about five or six policemen in the Logan detachment. These and twenty additional top men will be sufficient to convince that gang that the State means business. For my bodyguard I would like for you to direct the Superintendent to have Lieut. Frank Gibson report to me in the morning and remain with me as long as I desire. I shall use him as a contact man until the trial begins. I have known Gibson since he was a small boy in Bluefield. For cool courage he has no superior, and he is a powerful man physically. He was stationed in Logan a long time and knows all the crooks there, and they know him. No matter what the odds Red Gibson will never run away."

"All right," replied the Governor, "Gibson will be at your office in the morning. Let me know a day or so in advance and the twenty extra police will be in Logan the evening before the trial begins. Good luck."

Lieutenant Gibson reported at my office the next morning, and in the afternoon I sent him to Logan to:

1. File with Judge Jackson a copy of the Governor's letter directing me to prosecute Scaggs.

2. Serve on Enoch Scaggs in the jail a copy of a notice that three days later I would ask the court to call a jury from Monroe County to try him for the murder of Roy Knotts.

3. Serve a notice on the Prosecuting Attorney that, at the direction of the Governor, I was taking over the prosecution of Enoch Scaggs for the murder of Roy Knotts; and that henceforth neither he nor his assistant would have any official connection with the case.

Three days later Gibson drove me to Logan. The only business was to have a day set for Scaggs' trial, and to order a jury from Monroe County. Two State Police brought the prisoner from the jail, and a day was set for his trial to begin. I presented my motion for calling a jury from Monroe County, and the court order was promptly signed by the Judge requiring the attendance of forty prospective jurors from that county. A State Policeman was directed to deliver a copy of such order to the clerk of the Circuit Court of Monroe County forthwith, and Gibson and I returned to Charleston.

This was my first sight of Scaggs. His was the most sinister face I have ever seen. He was a moron, with a sardonic smile that made him absolutely repulsive.

On our way to Charleston I discussed with Gibson the probability of this Logan gang sending an emissary to Monroe County to attempt to bribe a few jurors. To meet this possibility I sent Gibson into that county the next morning to patrol the highways and intercept any approaching Logan "fixers." In the meantime the Governor had arranged with the Chesapeake and Ohio Railroad to have a special passenger coach placed on a siding at Ronceverte for the transportation of the forty jurors to Logan County. While in Monroe County, Gibson was to notify the jurors the day and hour of the departure of their train.

Sending Gibson to Monroe County was well timed. The

second day he saw a well-known Logan gangster driving toward Union, the county seat. Gibson stopped him and said: "I suppose you are up here to bribe a few jurors, as you do in Logan County. Well, you are not going to see any of them, for I am going to be right behind you every minute you are in this county. Now get going before you get hurt. I'll follow you to the county line, and don't come back." The order was promptly obeyed.

Chapter 18

THE TRIAL[1]

Gibson and I arrived in Logan in midafternoon, February 2, 1931, the day before the trial was to open. The twenty extra State Policemen were already there, and the forty prospective jurors from Monroe County, guarded by a State Trooper, arrived in a special coach attached to the regular six o'clock train. They were escorted to their quarters, the entire top floor of a local hotel, by a number of troopers, and kept under their watchful eyes throughout the night.

Our hotel room, which Lieutenant Gibson had engaged a few days earlier, was large, with two double beds. He took the one facing the door, and I the one in the corner farthest from the door. As a safety precaution, Red[2] suggested that he always answer a knock on the door, and also that he enter and leave the room first. In that way he could spot anyone hiding in the room, or lurking in the hallway. At bedtime he took an extra service pistol from his handbag, and laid it on my bed, and placed his own gun beside his pillow, with the remark: "Hope we won't need 'em; but, if we do need 'em, we got 'em." This was the routine every night we were in Logan.

About ten o'clock there was a light tap on our door. Cautiously, Red opened it, pistol in hand. Our caller was, so he said, an "old-timer" in Logan—"lived here a heap o' years." For an hour and a half he regaled us with horror stories of the lawlessness of the "gang," and the cruelty of "Killer Scaggs." "You know," he said, "Knotts is the fifth man Scaggs has murdered in Logan that I know about, and this is

---

[1] See Appendix I, Note 12, for statement of Judge Robert D. Bailey, who assisted me in the prosecution of Scaggs.

[2] Lieutenant Gibson was of a rather florid complexion and his hair had a tinge of red. Hence he was sometimes called "Red" by his friends, but this signified affection and respect. When he retired from the State Police, Red went back to his home county of Mercer. He has served two terms as justice of the peace, and is now (June, 1967) a member of the county court. Note: January 1, 1969, Red is still a member of the Court.

the first time he has been arrested. When Don Chafin was in power, Scaggs was one of his main men, and Chafin protected him. I don't know what the connection is between him and Sheriff Joe Hatfield. Maybe there ain't none, but it looks bad."

The next evening two other Old-Timers came furtively to see me. Their stories, for the most part, were repetitions of those heard the evening before. In the months he was stationed in Logan, Gibson had heard these stories many times, and he believed some of them were true. Later, I asked Judge Jackson about them and he replied: "Well, I am afraid that there is a grain of truth in some of them."

We had similar visitors nearly every evening we were in Logan, and none would leave until Gibson had gone through the hallway and made sure no one would see them leave my room. Usually, their parting words were a warning, such as: "Be careful, and remember this bunch will kill you if they think they can get by with it."

The first morning of the trial, before the general public was admitted to the courtroom, the jurors were brought in by State Police and seated in a section reserved for them. As the last juror entered, two State Troopers quickly blocked the doorway. A dozen State Police then moved in and took up advantageous positions, well scattered over the room. The door policemen then proceeded to search all persons for firearms as they entered. Even deputy sheriffs and tin-badge special constables were told to "park" their guns elsewhere, or they could not enter. This procedure was followed throughout the trial. A number of other troopers patrolled the immediate area surrounding the courthouse.

Accompanied by Gibson and two other troopers, I made my way through the milling crowd on the streets, past a dozen uniformed deputy sheriffs, and as many tin-badge special constables, and through the densely packed courtroom to the counsel table. There I found an old friend, Judge R. D. Bailey,' of Pineville, West Virginia, a former Circuit Judge

---

[3] This was the same Robert D. Bailey, who, as Judge of the Circuit Court of Mingo County, presided over the Matewan Massacre Trials in Williamson in 1921.

and a very able lawyer, who had been retained by relatives of the murdered chief of police to assist me in the prosecution. I also had the very able assistance of Hon. Claude A. Joyce, City Attorney of the Town of Logan, who had been directed by the city council to render every possible aid in the case.[4]

To our great surprise a twelve-man jury was quickly selected from the Monroe County group, and sworn to try the issue. Sitting a few feet behind me was Sheriff Hatfield, ready to name two of his deputies to have the care and custody of the jury during the trial, which, probably, would last a week. At this point I rose and said: "Your Honor, I have a motion to make at this time. For reasons known to the Court, I move that the care and custody of this jury during this trial be taken from Sheriff Hatfield and his deputies, and that your Honor name two reputable citizens of this county as special officers of the Court to perform that duty." The Court promptly sustained the motion, and named the special officers. Sheriff Hatfield left the room immediately, and I did not see him again during the trial.

The second morning of the trial the State Police reported to me that for several hours the night before Emmett Scaggs, assistant prosecuting attorney and a cousin of the defendant, had twelve to fifteen of the "tin-badge-special-constable" perjurers in a room over the bus station coaching and schooling them on what perjured testimony they were to give in the case. But there was nothing that I could do about it at the time.

In the early afternoon on the second day of the trial, the prosecution concluded its direct testimony and the perjurers took over. Their collective story was practically the same as predicted by Judge Jackson in his conversation with the Governor and me; that they were present and saw the shooting; that Knotts began to curse and abuse Scaggs and rushed at him and threw his hand to his hip pocket as if he were going

---

[4] Scaggs was defended by Mr. C. C. Chambers, a very able and honorable member of the Logan County Bar. For many years he has been, and is now (1967), Judge of the Logan County Circuit Court.

to draw a gun and "Mr. Scaggs shot him to protect himself." But under cross-examination they were no longer "professional perjurers," but sorry pictures of the lowest form of cowering, congenital liars.

In the old courthouse, the courtroom, witness rooms, and prosecuting attorney's office were on the second floor. Just under the second-story windows was a cornice that projected outward from the wall for 20 inches, wide enough for one to pass along it from window to window. Immediately after the defense began to present its testimony, a State Policeman told me that witnesses were leaving the witness room through a window, passing along this cornice to the prosecuting attorney's office, where Emmett Scaggs, assistant prosecutor, was giving them final instructions on how to give their perjured testimony. I sent Gibson to investigate. He took the office key from Scaggs, told him to leave the courthouse or he would be jailed and held for contempt of court, and put a State Policeman in charge of the office. We did not see the Assistant Prosecutor again. We were told that the Prosecuting Attorney got drunk the day before the trial began and went into seclusion. We did not see him at any time.

To destroy any favorable effect that this perjured testimony might have on the jury, I decided to show by their fellow townsmen that these hoodlums were unworthy of belief. So I subpoenaed twenty of the town's leading businessmen to appear forthwith as witnesses for the prosecution.

These witnesses were assembled in a room off the main courtroom. When I entered the room they were nervously excited, everybody talking, wondering why they were called. I clapped my hands for attention, and said: "First, let's all sit down and be comfortable. Next, I want you to calm down. There is nothing here to be nervous about. You people know these witnesses who have testified that Scaggs shot Knotts in self-defense. They are (here I read their names). You also know that these jurors are from Monroe County, and never heard of these professional perjurers; and if their story goes unchallenged, the jury might assume that it is true.

"Therefore," I said, "I have decided to impeach the credibility of these witnesses by their fellow townsmen, who know their general reputation for truth and veracity, and will testify that they would not believe them on oath." Then I gave these witnesses a clear explanation of the preliminary questions leading up to the final and decisive question, and explained what their answers should be. This done, I said to the man sitting nearest me: "Now, sir, will you so testify?" He got to his feet, began nervously to wring his hands, and haltingly answered: "Well, well, I don't know the gentlemen at all. I never had any business dealings with them, and I don't see. . ."

"Stop!" I interrupted. "Did you hear me say anything about business dealings? That has nothing to do with the issue. If you had had a business transaction with them, you would not be permitted to mention it. The truth is you have no *guts*. You are afraid to stand up and fight to clean up your city and county. You are excused. Get out!" He went out the door and I never saw him again. I disliked to be so harsh, but I assumed that attitude hoping to boost the morale of the other prospective witnesses.

I turned to the other witnesses and said: "Now, I want to tell you people something. I am not being paid one cent for my services in this case. I volunteered to come over here and help you. But if you don't have the guts to help yourselves, to stand up and fight to clean up your community, then I am sorry I came. I will walk out of this courthouse and leave you to swelter in this damn mess, and I'll never come into your county again."

The first to speak was Rev. Robert Coverlee, pastor of the First Baptist Church. He said: "I shall so testify. I am not afraid." Dr. S. B. Lawson, a prominent physician and owner of the local hospital, was the next to speak. He said: "Put my name down. I'll go through with it if they shoot me the next minute." He was followed by Dr. J. O. Hill, also a prominent physician; and they continued to speak up until we had a dozen volunteers. However, after he took the stand to testify, one witness was in such a state of near-collapse from fear that he was excused, and I had to assist him from the witness chair.

After he testified, Dr. Hill started to return to his office. Two of the impeached witnesses, Oscar and Freeland White, brothers, and special constables, were waiting for him near the courthouse. One began to curse the Doctor and threaten him. Hill made his way back into the courtroom and reported the incident to me. I turned to Gibson and said: "Red, go out and get those men, tear their badges off, take their guns, and lock them up." He was gone like a flash. I think that was the kind of action he had been hoping for. In a few minutes he was back with the laconic report: "The White brothers are in jail." At the noon recess I advised Judge Jackson of the incident. He remarked: "Let them sweat a few days." There was no more interference with witnesses.

While the jury was deliberating on its verdict, the Judge directed the State Police to bring the White brothers from the jail, and also to call Dr. Hill. Freeland White told the Judge that he was on probation in the Federal Court, and did not say a word to Dr. Hill. This was confirmed by the Doctor, and Freeland was dismissed. Oscar was adjudged guilty of contempt of court and sentenced to six months in jail. He served about four months of his sentence in Fayette County Jail and was released on probation.

The jury returned its verdict on February 7, four days after the trial began. Eleven jurors voted for murder in the first degree and the death penalty, but one juror hung out for second-degree murder. After a few hours the eleven other jurors agreed on the lesser crime, and the prisoner was sentenced to serve eighteen years in the penitentiary. He served his full sentence, less time off for good behavior, and died shortly after his release.[5]

[5] For many years Mr. Walter R. Thurmond was connected with the coal industry in Logan County and lived in the town of Logan. A few years after this trial the Governor appointed him on the State Board of Control, a body that had supervision and control of all State institutions. Mr. Thurmond later told me that on his first visit to the penitentiary he learned that the warden had made a "trusty" of Scaggs and put him out on the prison farm. Mr. Thurmond had known Scaggs for years, and knew that he was a dangerous, heartless killer—unfit to be at large. Immediately, he directed the warden to return Scaggs to the prison and to keep him within its walls during the remainder of his sentence.

Chapter 19

END OF LOGAN'S MINE GUARDS[1]

The trial over, Gibson and I drove back to Charleston between two cars filled with State Police who were returning to their respective posts. I instructed Gibson, however, to remain in Charleston, as I might have some additional work for him.

Two days later I filed my report with the Governor, and made the following specific recommendations:

1. That the State Police be ordered by the Governor to prevent any future operation of slot machines in Logan County.

2. That the Governor direct the Sheriff of Logan County to dismiss, at once, all company-paid deputy sheriffs and other mine guards.

3. That the Governor notify all justices of the peace in Logan County to revoke, at once, the appointment of all their special constables, and to make no more such appointments.

4. Should the Sheriff or any justice of the peace refuse to obey such orders, I urge that they be impeached and removed for malfeasance in office.

5. Should the Governor approve these suggestions, and desire the assistance of the Attorney General's Office in implementing them, we shall welcome the assignment.

The Governor agreed with the suggestions, and directed me to begin the "cleanup" of Logan County immediately. The next morning I sent Lieutenant Gibson to Logan to deliver to Sheriff Hatfield a copy of my report to the Governor, a copy of the Governor's letter to me directing the "cleanup," and a brief letter from me, informing the Sheriff that if he desired to discuss the matter with me, I would see him in my office the next morning at ten o'clock.

The slot machines were hidden after Knotts was murdered,

[1] See Appendix I, Note 11, for statement by State Policeman Frank Gibson.

and I instructed Gibson to look over the town and see if they were being operated. He reported that they were not in use, and that one man who had had two machines in his place of business told him that they were not going to operate them "as long as the heat was on in the county."

Sheriff Hatfield arrived on the hour, accompanied by his big 200-pound chief deputy (whose name I have forgotten). When I was in Logan, I was told by the State Police and numerous other persons, that this deputy was thoroughly disliked and distrusted by the public and generally regarded as the architect of most of the Sheriff's troubles.

"Well, Sheriff," I said, "I suppose you want to talk to me about my report to the Governor?"

"Yes," he replied, "that is what I came to talk to you about."

"What do you want to do about it?" I queried.

"General," he answered, "I want to make a good sheriff, and if you will not impeach me I'll let you and Governor Conley run the sheriff's office. I'll do anything you say."

"Joe, that sounds all right," I replied, "but you may not be able to do what we will ask. They may have so much on you that you can't do it."

"Nobody has anything on me," was his spirited reply.

"All right, Sheriff, we will go along with you for the present," I said. "The first thing I shall ask you to do is to dismiss that man sitting right there (pointing to his chief deputy). I think that he has ceased to serve either your interest, or the interest of the people of Logan County."

The Sheriff walked over and took the deputy's badge, lifted his gun, and said: "Report to the office tomorrow and get your salary to date." Without a word the deputy walked out of my office and I never saw him again.

"Sheriff," I said, "the Governor and I have worked out a plan which you must follow, absolutely." I outlined the following:

1. You must dismiss and disarm every deputy sheriff you have whose salary is paid by the Logan County Coal Operators Association, or by any coal company.

2. The same is true of every deputy where you pay his salary with money contributed to you by the same association, or by individual operators.

3. You must disarm all special constables in the county, have their appointments revoked by the justices who made them, and notify the justices not to make such appointments in the future. If any justice refuses to obey your orders, you will notify me at once, and I will start proceedings to remove him from office.

4. You are to have only the deputies whose salaries are paid by the county, not to exceed eight in number.

5. If the county will not pay the salaries of eight deputies, you will reduce the number accordingly.

6. In no case will you retain or appoint as a deputy sheriff any individual who served as a deputy under former Sheriff Don Chafin.

7. You will furnish me immediately a list of twenty individuals from which you are to select your eight deputies. We will check the list and strike from it the name of any individual you may not retain or appoint.

8. You will notify the owners of all slot machines in Logan County that they have 48 hours, from and after six o'clock tomorrow evening, to remove them from the county; and any machine found in the county after that time will be seized and destroyed by the State Police.

Sheriff Hatfield accepted every provision of the plan, and left at once for Logan to prepare the list of names I requested.

In the meantime, I had mailed a copy of my report on Logan County to the late James D. Francis, executive vice-president and active manager of the Island Creek Coal Company, and requested him to come to my office for a conference at ten o'clock the morning after Sheriff Hatfield was to come.

The Island Creek Coal Company was then, and is now, the largest producer in the county, and one of the most progressive companies in the State. Mr. Francis was humane and fair with his workers, a devout churchman—an outstanding example of a Christian industrialist. Moreover, he was a leader among the operators and I knew that if I could win him to my side the fight would be much easier.

Mr. Francis arrived on the hour, accompanied by another Logan County operator, whose name I do not now recall. I read to them the Governor's letter directing the cleanup of Logan County. I also told them of Sheriff Hatfield's visit the day before, of the dismissal of his chief deputy, of the plan the Governor and I had worked out, and of the Sheriff's acceptance of that plan.

And then I said:

"Gentlemen, that is our plan and our purpose. I have invited you here to inquire whether you will cooperate with us in this too long delayed effort to clean up Logan County. If you will not, then I want to know it now."

In substance, Mr. Francis replied:

"Mr. Lee, if you can and will carry out this plan, it will be the greatest favor to the Logan County coal operators you could possibly do them. This deputy-sheriff system began several years ago, before I came to the county. It was small then, and the operators controlled it. Now it is large, and it controls the operators. We are helpless. We have no voice in the selection of these deputies, and no control over them. If we should try to fire one or quit paying, it is more than likely that they would toss a bomb into our mine or burn a tipple. These fellows are powerful, they are organized, and they are ruthless. But with the power and authority of the State in your hands, and with the Sheriff cooperating, I don't see how you can fail. We are with you in this effort, and we will cooperate as far as we can without endangering our property."

The next day a couple of other Logan operators called to see me. After a few complimentary remarks on the outcome of the Scaggs trial, one said: "General, you have that bunch whipped, they are on the run; and for God's sake don't weaken and don't let the Governor weaken. For years that bunch of gangsters has bled us white financially. We made Don Chafin a millionaire, and when we revolted and threw him out and put in another sheriff, all we got was just a change in the general manager—no change in personnel or method of operation. The same gangsters have continued to bleed us and are still doing so. We operators do not dare fire one of them or quit paying without running a great risk of having our property destroyed. You have the cleanup started, and we are counting on you to finish the job."

The following day I received Sheriff Hatfield's list of names. While I was in Logan Judge Jackson gave me the names of twenty citizens of Logan (ten Democrats and ten Republicans) who would assist me in any way possible. A copy of the Sheriff's list with a letter of explanation was delivered by Lieutenant Gibson to each of these individuals with the request that they write me, in confidence, their unbiased opinion of the fitness of each man for the position of deputy sheriff. I also consulted Gibson, who knew personally many of the individuals named. It was the consensus that the Sheriff's selections were good ones; so I notified him that he might select any eight on the list. Thus surrendered the greater part of the "Standing Army of Logan."

In the meantime Sheriff Hatfield carried out our understanding to the letter. The slot machines left the county within the time limit I had fixed. The Sheriff freed himself of the company-paid, trouble-making deputy sheriffs and rid the county of its infestation of tin-badge irresponsible special constables. And the reports of the State Police showed that for the remainder of his term Joe Hatfield made an excellent sheriff and the county, probably, enjoyed the most peaceful era of its troubled history.

The Attorney General's Office has none of the inquisitional powers of a grand jury. Therefore, I never questioned Sheriff Joe Hatfield about his reputed connection with the slot-machine racket; neither did I ever tell him what Judge Jackson had reported to the Governor and me. I simply did the job assigned me by the Governor and, under the law, I could go no further. However, the State Police were never able to establish any connection between the Sheriff and Scaggs; nor were they ever able to ascertain the motive that prompted Scaggs in his murderous act.

During the trial I talked with a prominent Logan physician about Scaggs. The doctor had known him casually for some years and had treated him professionally on a few occasions. He regarded Scaggs as a man of low mentality, and an alcoholic. "Judging from his homicidal tendencies," said the doctor, "I would say that he is now, and probably has been since childhood, criminally insane, and should have been permanently isolated from society in his youth. It is possible that in his warped mind he resented having one he regarded as a 'furriner' as chief of police in his home town.'"

At the session of the Legislature following the trial, I prepared and the lawmakers enacted a statute which prohibits justices of the peace from appointing special constables and giving them authority to carry pistols. This law permanently demobilized the remainder of the "Standing Army of Logan."

The dismissal of the Logan mine guards, however, had no effect upon their continued use in other coal counties. But in their 1934 labor contract with the now legalized union the operators agreed to abolish the whole mine-guard system. A few sheriffs, however, said that they were not parties to that contract and refused to dismiss such deputies.

But shortly thereafter Governor H. G. Kump ordered those dissident sheriffs to disarm and dismiss their mine-guard deputies, or he would send the State Police to do it for them. The sheriffs reluctantly obeyed, and that action ended the long and brutal rule of the hated mine guards in West Virginia's coal fields.

As strange as it may now seem, after 1913, all mine guard deputies were appointed and operated in direct violation of law. In that year, while the Cabin Creek and Paint Creek

---

[2] With many of the native mountain folk a "furriner" may come from "cross the mountain," or from another county or state, or from "cross the water."

strike was at its worst, the Legislature passed an act which made it unlawful for sheriffs to appoint such deputy mine guards, but the statute was wholly ignored. The coal operators continued to name the sheriffs in the coal counties, and the sheriffs continued to appoint the operators' gunmen as deputies, in defiance of the law.

Again, following the 1921-1922 strike in Mingo County, the Legislature attempted to abolish the mine-guard system, by amending the existing law. But this statute was regarded as a legislative jest by both coal operators and sheriffs, and mine guards continued to rule the coal fields.

"How was it," I once asked the late Jess Sullivan, secretary of the West Virginia Coal Operators Association, "that the coal companies and sheriffs were able to disregard the 1913 and 1921 laws forbidding the appointment of mine guards as deputy sheriffs?"

"Those statutes were passed long before I became connected with the coal industry, but I have heard their stories many times," said he. "Both laws were passed just after strikes. The politicians thought that something had to be done to pacify the miners; but the operators saw to it that neither law carried any penalty for its violation."

It was not until 1935 that the Legislature added the long omitted penalty—a fine of $500, or one year in jail for any sheriff who appoints such mine guards as deputy sheriffs.

Part Five

REVOLT IN THE NORTH[1]

West Virginia's mine wars were not confined to her southern mountains. Due to the early construction of the Baltimore and Ohio Railroad, her northern coal fields in the valleys of the Tygart, West Fork, Cheat, and Monongahela rivers were the first to be developed. These regions were the first to suffer from the disastrous effects of the seemingly irrepressible conflicts between the coal operators and their miners; nor did the passing years lessen the number or abate the fury of those labor wars. The strike described here was the last major disturbance in the field. It began October 10, 1924, and lasted four years—until it ruined the miners' union and broke many of the coal companies in the valleys.

[1] The whole of Part Five is based upon the evidence taken by and report of the Senate Gooding Committee that investigated this strike, various court records, evidence heard at the trials of the criminal strikers, reports of the State Police, and my personal observations and experiences during a number of visits to the strike zone.

Chapter 20

OPERATORS REPUDIATE THEIR UNION CONTRACT[1]

With few exceptions, West Virginia's northern mines operated nonunion until the summer of 1916, when the entire northern field was unionized as a result of the political ambitions and machinations of the late Clarence W. Watson, head of the Consolidation Coal Company, the largest producer in the field.

In January, 1911, Watson visited the State Capitol, "armed with a fountain pen and a checkbook," said a Charleston newspaper, and an appreciative Legislature clothed him with the toga of a United States Senator for an unexpired term of two years. But in 1913 the political complexion of the Legislature had changed, and he was succeeded by Nathan Goff, a Republican.

In 1916 Watson was the Democratic nominee for the U. S. Senate. In the meantime, however, the XVII Amendment to the Constitution had been adopted, and he was obliged to submit his candidacy to the voters instead of the Legislature.

Always, Watson had been an uncompromising foe of labor unions, but political expediency now required that he placate these groups. It was openly charged at the time that he made a deal with the miners' union, in which, in return for its political support, he signed an agreement that resulted in the unionization of all miners in this northern field. But in the eyes of his fellow operators, he was guilty of a gross betrayal of their common cause, and they defeated him in the November election. The Senator's conversion to unionism, however, was insincere, and he waited only for an opportunity to strike it a deadly blow.

In former years, many efforts were made to unionize these northern miners; but always they were crushed by county

[5] See Appendix I, Notes 13 and 14.

officers and mine guards. Van A. Bittner, a union official, once told me that many times he and other union organizers had stood in the public highways and shouted their appeals to groups of miners who, fearful of being assaulted by mine guards, cowered out of sight in the underbrush.

Always, the operators had contended that the miners' union was an unincorporated association of irresponsible individuals that broke its contracts at will, and left them without recourse. Be that as it may, the fact is that the long and disastrous mine war of 1924-1929, which brought hunger, suffering, and disease to the workers, and financial ruin to many of the coal companies in the strike district, was the direct result of the repudiation by the operators of a wage agreement between them and the union.

That contract, effective April 1, 1924, to March 31, 1927, known as the "Baltimore Agreement," was entered into by the representatives of the coal companies and the miners' union, ratified by both parties, and put into effect.

Six months later, however, the coal operators one by one began to repudiate their solemn covenant. The first to welsh was the Bethlehem Steel Company, which operated a number of "captive mines"[2] in the district. It was followed by Senator Watson's Consolidation Coal Company, the largest in the field. Others followed rapidly until every company in the area except four had repudiated their union contract.

The operators gave no explanation of and offered no excuse for that wanton violation of their pledged word. They refused to enter into any discussion with union representatives, and even declined to confer with the Secretary of Labor, who sought to settle the trouble.

In 1928, however, in testifying before the Gooding Senate Committee,[3] a number of operators attempted to justify their action on two grounds: (a) that the union agreement was signed by their association, and not by the individual

---

[2] In the trade, a "captive mine" is one where the entire output of the mine is used in the owner's own mills and factories.
[3] See Appendix I, Note 13.

companies, and later they withdrew from their association, and, therefore, they were no longer bound by the contract; and (b) that coal prices had been so reduced that repudiation of the agreement was necessary if the coal companies were to continue in business.

The first excuse is the same as saying that, after a partnership has incurred obligations, one partner may escape liability by simply withdrawing from the firm, or that all may escape by dissolving the partnership; while the second is equivalent to saying that an anticipated loss will justify the repudiation of business contracts.

But neither contention was sustained by the facts. The Bethlehem Steel Company sold no coal on the open market, but consumed its entire output in its own steel mills. And the evidence before the Senate Committee showed that the four companies that stood by their union agreement operated at a profit during the entire strike period.

The first that the miners knew of the repudiation of their union agreement was when the coal companies posted notices on the bulletin boards at their plants announcing that after a certain day the mines would be closed unless the workers agreed to work nonunion and accepted a substantial reduction in wages.

To meet the expected violent reaction from the miners, the operators employed additional mine guards, erected high barbed wire fences around their mines, posted watchmen at the gates to exclude unwanted visitors, installed searchlights at strategic points, procured a supply of high-power rifles and ammunition, and waited for the coming storm to strike.

For many years these northern companies had maintained their own private guards and deputy sheriffs. But, faced with a strike of major proportions, they deemed it prudent to import a few "peace officers" from the southern mountains. Among these imported guards were a score, or more, of the most notorious of the Baldwin-Felts thugs headed by Buster Pence and Everett Lively, two of the assassins of Sid Hatfield and Ed Chambers on the courthouse steps in Welch.[4] They were brought in to teach the less experienced northern gentry the "gentle art of refined brutality."

The operators next resorted to the old Red Jacket Yellow-Dog Contract, but they added a new flourish to it. The last sentence implored the operators "for the sake of the workers" to reopen their mines "even at reduced wages."

One by one the miners were called in and told to sign one of these "death warrants," as the miners called them, or else to vacate his company owned house and get off company property within twenty-four hours.

Faced with starvation and intimidated by mine guards, probably one fourth of the miners signed these Yellow-Dog Contracts. But approximately twenty thousand refused to surrender their contract rights, and on October 10, 1924, they walked off their jobs in what proved to be the most prolonged and disastrous strike ever waged in the State. As new scab miners were employed they, too, were required to sign the same Yellow-Dog Contracts.

In accordance with the terms of their house leases, and with a ruthlessness never surpassed in the southern mountains, the operators began to evict all strikers from their company-owned shanties.

Eventually, conditions became so deplorable that in 1928 the U. S. Senate appointed a committee, headed by Senator Frank R. Gooding, of Idaho, to investigate this whole strike situation.[5] A number of witnesses testified—operators, strikers, union leaders—and scores of strikers filed their affidavits with the Committee, all of which graphically described one of the blackest chapters in the industrial history of the Nation.

But as usual, nothing came of the investigation.

[4] See Chapter 9.
[5] See Appendix I, Notes 13 and 14.

Chapter 21

ONE-SIDED INJUNCTIONS

When starvation failed to crush the strikers' resistance, the operators resorted to the injunction. John L. Lewis, president of the miners' union, Van A. Bittner, district president, and a number of local union leaders, were hailed before the U. S. District Court, charged with the violation of an old injunction issued ten years earlier; but they were found "not guilty" and discharged.

Impressed by the results obtained by their southern neighbors in the famous Red Jacket Case, the operators resorted to court action on their Yellow-Dog Contracts. Injunctions were obtained in the Circuit Court of Monongalia County inhibiting the union or its agents "by any means whatsoever from interfering with plaintiffs' mines, or by enticement or persuasion, causing their employees to leave their service or preventing other persons from entering their service."

For a speech made to a group of strikers in an adjoining county, before notice of the injunction had been served on him, Van Bittner was adjudged guilty of contempt of court, fined $500, and sentenced to serve six months in jail. But the State's Supreme Court set aside the conviction and discharged the accused.[1] Many others, however, were not so fortunate, and during the strike years the county jails in the area were kept filled with the victims of that one-sided method of dispensing justice.

In the meantime the union leaders decided that if they could be enjoined from inducing scab workers to break their Yellow-Dog Contracts, the coal operators also could be enjoined from breaking their wage agreement with the union. They presented a petition to the Circuit Court of Monongalia County praying for an injunction to restrain one of the coal companies from operating its mines in violation of its union agreement.

---

[1] See *State vs. Bittner*, 102 West Virginia Supreme Court Reports, page 677.

They soon learned, however, that in that jurisdiction injunctions were for coal companies only. In a lengthy opinion, remarkable for its exhibition of judicial prejudice against the miners' union and its officials rather than for its depth of sound legal reasoning, Judge I. Grant Lazelle, of the Circuit Court of Monongalia County, denied the injunction on the grounds that the contract between the operators and the union was "so involved, technical, and ambiguous as to be beyond my comprehension."

The Judge's opinion of the contract was in strange contrast with the testimony of George Anderson, executive vice-president of the Consolidation Coal Company, before the U. S. Senate Committee. Anderson was one of the representatives of the operators at the Baltimore Wage Conference where this agreement was prepared, agreed to, and signed by the operators' association and the union.

"It was a collective labor agreement," said Anderson, "a perfectly ordinary and common variety of contractual relationship between thousands of men on one side, working through their union, and hundreds of operators on the other, working through their union, or operators' association. Both parties entered into this agreement, both parties ratified it through their agents, and it went into effect."

But self-interest had biased the judgment and blinded the judicial discernment of the learned Judge, and wholly disqualified him as judge in any legal proceedings growing out of the strike. The evidence before the Gooding Senate Committee showed that at the time of the injunction hearings, he and his family were the lessors of one of the interested coal companies and were then receiving, and had received since 1920, a large sum annually in coal royalties, which in one year amounted to $60,000. When this fact developed, His Honor excused the stain on his judicial ermine by the simple explanation that "the matter had entirely escaped my memory at the time of the hearings."

Completely strangled by injunctions, the strikers became outcasts, driven to desperation by cruelty and hunger. But unlike their mountain brethren to the south, only in isolated

Strikers' forts at Grant Town.

instances did they resort to the rifle and machine gun. Many suffered in dumb and unresisting silence; some disavowed their union obligations, resumed their old jobs, and began to sabotage from within; while on the outside the more daring began a systematic destruction of property seldom equaled in industrial conflicts. Mines were blown up, railroad trestles and coal tipples destroyed, homes of strikebreakers bombed, and a reign of terror was created in the district.

In some camps a large number of strikers were of foreign birth and varying nationalities. They had come to this "land of promise" to escape the earthbound drudgery of restless Europe only to find themselves hopelessly buried in America's black pits and embroiled in her endless labor wars. Many of them could neither speak nor understand the English language, and were highly susceptible to radical influences. They regarded the scab workers as public enemies, and believed that the strike should be conducted in the same manner as their Balkan wars.

About five hundred strikers, mostly foreigners, had been employed in a mine at Grant Town, Marion County, and still lived in the village. This polyglot group decided to wipe out the local scabs in a massacre so horrible as to strike terror to the hearts of the other strikebreakers in the district.

A large number of high-power rifles and a supply of ammunition were secretly brought into camp. The union hall, located near the mine entrance, was converted into a fortress by cutting portholes through the walls and lining the inside with heavy tile and bags of cement. By working secretly at night, the strikers constructed a number of bullet-proof "forts" on the wooded hillside overlooking the mine. Their intention was to fill these strongholds with men armed with rifles and shoot down the scabs as they left the mine mouth at four o'clock in the afternoon.

But a native American striker betrayed their plans to the officers, and, shortly after noon on the day fixed for the slaughter, forty State Police arrived in the village, seized the hail, destroyed the "forts," and prevented the tragedy. The rifles were never found.

Chapter 22

SABOTAGE

On March 4, 1925, Howard M. Gore was inaugurated Governor of West Virginia, and I became the State's Attorney General. This northern strike had been in progress for five months and was growing more bitter each day. A few days after taking office the Governor called his new Superintendent of State Police, Col. R. E. O'Connor, and me to his office to discuss the strike situation.

The Governor was from Clarksburg, located in the heart of the strike district, and thoroughly familiar with conditions in the area. He informed us that the strikers had stolen sixteen 2-gallon cans of nitroglycerine from an oil company, and a number of 5-gallon cans of blasting powder and a quantity of dynamite from a coal company. "The criminal element among the strikers," he said, "have used some of these explosives to destroy or damage mines, railroad trestles, and the homes of non-striking miners. But much of it is still in their hands. The people of the district are frightened. They don't know where or when these criminals will strike next."

The Governor ordered Colonel O'Connor to put a dozen of his best men in plain clothes and keep them on the case until the criminals were caught. He also directed me to take personal charge of all prosecutions when they were once in custody.

The next morning the Superintendent of State Police and I went to Fairmont, in the strike area. We soon learned of the presence in the district of the strikebreaking Baldwin-Felts mine guards, headed by the notorious Buster Pence and Everett Lively.

Under the provisions of their house leases, the operators had ordered their mine guards to evict all strikers from their company-owned shanties. Along the highways we saw many small groups of women and children keeping watch over their meager household belongings, where they had been dumped by mine guards. Both women and children were haggard, poorly clad, hungry, and cold. They were waiting for the return of husbands and fathers with trucks to remove their belongings to the barrack towns erected by the union to house the outcasts.

Barrack town of striking miners in northern field.

That evening I recommended to the Governor by telephone that he direct Colonel O'Connor to notify the Baldwin-Felts guards to leave the district at once; and that he order the State Police to prevent further evictions, except when ordered by the courts.

The Governor gave the orders, and the Colonel so notified the secretary of the local Coal Operators Association that night. The next morning the Baldwin-Felts guards packed their guns and left for the more congenial atmosphere of their southern mountains.

But the Governor's order to halt evictions only postponed the evil days. Court orders were soon obtained, and groups of heavily armed local mine guards carried out the court orders with the pitilessness of Russian Cossacks. During the first few months of the strike no fewer than thirty thousand men, women, and children were driven from their homes, and their household goods strewn along the village streets and highways.

To provide shelter for that homeless multitude, the union

hastily erected numerous barrack towns in which it housed and fed the victims of that industrial madness during the four agonizing strike years that followed.

Three disastrous mine explosions occurred in the district during the strike. The first, March 17, 1925, at Barrackville, Marion County, completely destroyed the mine and took a toll of 35 lives; the second, January 14, 1926, at Farmington, Marion County, killed 19 miners; and a third, one of the State's major disasters, April 30, 1927, at Everettville, Monongalia County, took the lives of 97 workers. Also, a mine in Barbour County was blown up at night without any loss of life.

At the direction of the Governor, the Superintendent of State Police and I arrived at Everettville only a few hours after the explosion. It was a harrowing, heartbreaking experience. A small area around the mine entrance had been roped off to prevent the crowds from hampering rescue efforts. Outside this restricted area the wives and children of the entombed men kept tearful and ceaseless vigil. While standing in this group I heard a thoughtful rescue worker suggest to an expectant mother, who had been waiting hopefully for several hours, that she should go home and get some rest. "Oh!" she said, "I must be here when he is brought out." And, stifling a sob, she prayed aloud: "Oh! God, please bring him out alive."

Again and again rescue teams tried to enter the wrecked mine, only to be driven back by the deadly gas. The third day the ventilating fans were back in operation, and rescuers entered that ghastly charnel house. "All dead," was the signal flashed to the outside. And kindly hands led the frantic widows and weeping children back to their desolate shanties.

The great force of the explosion was through the main entry toward the mine mouth. With clothes burned away and charred beyond recognition, many bodies were found in this passageway. They were hanging from mine ribs, draped around support pillars, pressed against mine walls, buried under wreckage, and mangled beyond all belief—eyeballs blown from sockets, abdomens torn open and bowels strewn over the mine floor, heads smashed like overripe fruit, collapsed lungs, crushed chests, arms and legs torn from bodies. But most of the dead were found in the workrooms, out of the direct path of the explosion. And the contorted bodies and distorted faces showed how they died—victims of the deadly carbon monoxide gas generated by the explosion.

The bodies were far back under the hills, possibly a mile and a half, or even farther, from the mine entrance, and it took hours to clear a path through the wreckage for the stretcherbearers. Finally, the first body was brought out; and for interminable hours, it seemed, volunteers carried out bodies and laid them in rows on the ground, and covered them with black cloths, to await the arrival of State-supplied coffins.

It was there that I saw exhibited that snarling animal hatred felt by members of the miners' union for nonunion miners. Not far from the scene of the tragedy, on privately owned land, was a large barrack-like structure built by the union to house strikers and their families. Apparently, these former workers believed that the explosion was a form of divine punishment meted out to the scab miners who had taken their jobs. And, with a heartlessness akin to savagery, they and their wives would pass nearby and curse and jeer the grief-stricken women and children as they hopefully waited; nor did the death announcement calm their fury or abate their hatred. As bodies were brought to the surface, they sang ribald songs, and frequently used such vile utterances as "There's another goddamned strikebreakin' scab son-of-a-bitch gone straight to hell."

The operators claimed that the three mine explosions in the strike area were the crimes of the lawless element among the strikers. The union leaders replied that they were the natural results of the employment of inexperienced miners, and a lack of proper safety precautions. With the exception of the Everettville disaster, which was caused by the refusal of the mine owners to rock-dust their mine, circumstances strongly confirmed the suspicions of the operators.

Natural gas frequently accumulated in mines in the strike area, and to provide for its escape, holes had been drilled from the surface directly into the destroyed mines at Barrackville and Farmington. The operators said that the strikers blew up these two mines by dropping nitroglycerine bombs through these vents. But no evidence was offered at the inquests to sustain their contention.[1]

But, in 1928, in Monongah Mine in Marion County, a dastardly attempt was made to commit mass murder.[2] A young motorman moving his coal train to the tipple was stopped by a red light. In the rays of his headlight he saw two cans of the stolen nitroglycerine (previously referred to) beside a mine pillar. Badly frightened, he started running toward the mine entrance, a mile away.

Outside, the lad breathlessly told his story to the superintendent, who took a few volunteers and entered the mine to investigate. In addition to the two cans of nitroglycerine, they also found two 5-gallon cans of blasting powder, and twelve sticks of dynamite—enough explosives to have killed every worker in the mine.

Detonating caps had been inserted into two sticks of the dynamite, and a 50-foot slow-burning fuse attached to each cap. Both fuses had been lighted. One had burned to within twelve feet, and the other to within six feet of the explosives. A tragedy too horrible to even contemplate had been prevented by a coil of each fuse falling into a puddle of water.

In the meantime, the Superintendent of State Police as-

---

[1] At the direction of the Governor, I attended the coroner's inquest in Morgan-town on the Everettville explosion. The Chief of the State's Department of Mines, experts from the United States Bureau of Mines, and a number of competent mining engineers testified that the disaster was due solely to the failure or refusal of the mine owners to rock-dust their mine. The superintendent of the mine testified that for months prior to the explosion he had tried, without success, to secure from the nonresident owners of the mine an appropriation for rockdusting.

It is entirely possible that both the Barrackville and Farmington mine explosions were also due to the neglect or refusal of the mine owners to rock-dust their mines.

[2] This was a large mine and worked about four hundred miners on each shift.

signed two plainclothes men to work exclusively on the Barbour County explosion. Also, he sent ten undercover agents into the strike district. The regular police in the field were directed to follow up any leads they had, and to continue their regular police duties.

Chapter 23

ARRESTS AND CONFESSIONS

In the destroyed mine in Barbour County a few openings, large enough for a man to crawl through, had been dug from the interior of the mine to the surface to permit natural gas to escape. After the explosion, the State Police found a pocket knife in one of these vents, presumably lost by the criminal who planted the explosive. Inside the wrecked mine, they also found a fragment of one of the stolen nitroglycerine cans.

With these meager clues, the police went to work. One by one they checked and eliminated all former employees of the company except two young strikers who could not be found. The company's records showed only their names, ages, and when they began working—not where they were from.

Dressed in plain clothes, a State Trooper took the knife and began visiting the country schools of Barbour and adjoining counties. At recess and noon periods he would mingle with the children, show them the knife, tell them he had found it and wanted to return it to the owner, and ask if any of them recognized it.

The search kept up for weeks without results. Finally, when the trooper was about to give up the quest, he stopped at a small country school in Taylor County, showed the knife to the children, and made his usual statement. A small boy spoke up: "I know that knife," he said, "it belongs to my brother." The officer went home with the child; and the brother, a lad 17 years old, quickly identified the knife as one he had traded to one of the wanted strikers. "When I traded him the knife he lived out near Grafton," said the boy, "but he worked in a mine in Barbour County."

The officer transferred his search to the city of Grafton, and eventually found the wanted man's parents. He posed as a striker-friend of their son, and wanted to join him and try to get a job. But the parents were canny, and told him to leave his name and address, and, when they heard from their son, they would write him.

The trooper noticed a letter addressed to them lying on the table, and adroitly slipped it into his pocket. Away from the house he opened it. It was from the son and gave his street address in Newark, New Jersey. Leaving another trooper in the house to prevent the parents from communicating with their son, he hurried to Newark and arrested the wanted man. In his room was a letter from his associate in the bombing that gave his address in Brooklyn, New York. Leaving his prisoner in jail in Newark, he rushed to Brooklyn and arrested the other criminal. The prisoners were returned to Barbour County and lodged in jail to await trial.

Shortly thereafter, a break came in Marion County. An investigator reported that a young Italian striker, said to be an expert in the use of explosives, was running arms and ammunition into the strike district from Pittsburgh. He was put under 24-hour surveillance. Early one morning this striker left his home in Fairmont by automobile and headed north on Route 19. Immediately, two State Police in plain clothes and driving a car with Maryland license, pulled onto the highway and followed him to Pittsburgh—seventy-five miles distant.

On a side street, they watched the Italian carry a number of heavy boxes out of a basement and load them into his car. He then drove south on the same Route 19 highway toward West Virginia, followed by the officers. At Washington, Pennsylvania, the police telephoned State Police at Morgantown that the suspect was headed in their direction, and they continued to follow their quarry.

A mile inside West Virginia the police set up an impassable roadblock, and soon the expected car arrived. The Italian stopped and tried to turn, but was rammed by the police car following him. Officers rushed the suspect, dragged him from his car, handcuffed him, shoved him into a police car, and made him lie on the floor between the seats so that passing strikers would not see him. The boxes were quickly transferred to a police car, and a trooper drove the prisoner's car to a previously arranged hiding place. Three officers, with the prisoner, headed back through Pennsylvania toward Wheeling, West Virginia. The boxes contained high-power rifles and thousands of rounds of ammunition.

They had hardly got started when the prisoner became hysterical and began to beg the officers not to kill him. After calming him by assurances that he would not be hurt, they asked him why he thought they would kill him. The union bosses, he said, had told him he would be killed if the police caught him.

At Wheeling the police took the prisoner to a restaurant for supper before putting him in jail. This was repeated each evening, and on the fourth day he suddenly said: "You nice people. You no let union bosses kill me, me tell you plenty." The officers took him to their headquarters and, after being assured of the complete protection of the State Police, he told them how he and a notorious labor firebrand named Jim Toney[1] had stolen the nitroglycerine, dynamite, and powder, and had used much of it to destroy coal tipples, railroad trestles, and homes of scab miners.

Two cans of the nitroglycerine and a few sticks of dynamite, he said, were given to two Barbour County strikers to blow up a mine in that county. He admitted that he and Toney planted the explosive in the Monongah mine. He also disclosed that they had hidden seven cans of the nitroglycerine—five cans in "some woods" near Canonsburg, Pennsylvania, and two cans in "some bushes" near Weirton, West Virginia. He strongly denied, however, that he and Toney had any connection with the explosion in either the Barrackville or Farmington mine.

Accompanied by an explosives expert from the oil company and the prisoner, the State Police went to Canonsburg and recovered the five cans of nitroglycerine hidden near that city. Next, they proceeded to Weirton and picked up the two

[1] This was the same Jim Toney who led the mobs that destroyed the mining camp of Willis Branch in southern West Virginia. See Appendix II.

cans hidden there. The expert departed with his perilous load and the police returned to Wheeling with the prisoner.

A double obligation now rested upon the State Police to protect the prisoner. They must make certain of his testimony against Jim Toney; and they must prevent him from being murdered by union killers. For these reasons they kept him under constant guard and moved him to a different jail every few days.[2]

The anxiety of the union bosses in Fairmont increased daily. They knew that the Italian left Pittsburgh with the guns and ammunition; he had not arrived in Fairmont, and his car had not been found.

To learn definitely whether the police had the Italian, the union leaders persuaded his wife to permit their lawyer to use her name in a *habeas corpus* proceeding before the Supreme Court. The writ was issued, requiring the State Police to bring the prisoner into court and show why he was being detained, and why he should not be released on bail.

When the Superintendent of State Police came into court with the prisoner, his wife and union lawyer rushed over to him, but he shoved them away and repeated over and over: "Go way, go way, me no talk to you." The union attorney presented his case—that the prisoner was arrested for a bailable offense, had not been given a hearing, was being held *incommunicado*, and asked that he be admitted to bail.

The Court asked the Italian what he had to say.

Instantly, the prisoner was on his feet, greatly agitated, and talked in his broken English for fully ten minutes. Pointing his finger at the union lawyer, he said: "He lie. Me no hire him. He not my lawyer. My wife, she good woman. She no understand. I no tell her to do this. Union bosses have her do this. They want me out so they kill me. So I no swear against Toney. Toney he guilty. He do all I say. Me tell 'em truth. Me

---

[2] The preceding facts related in this chapter were given to me by Colonel R. E. O'Connor, then head of the State Police.

want to stay with State Police. Me safe with them. Me out, union bosses they kill me."[3]

The Court left the prisoner with the State Police. The union attorney tried to explain his appearance in the case by saying that "the matter had been misrepresented to him."

In due time the Barbour County criminals were convicted and sent to the penitentiary. Jim Toney also was convicted and sent to the penitentiary for a number of years. The union furnished them with able counsel in the trial court, but it made no effort to appeal their cases—they were expendable. Later, the Italian was deported by the immigration authorities.

But the removal of these criminals did not end the strike. It dragged wearily into the economic debacle of 1929—four long years—and ended with the collapse of the coal industry in the valleys. A number of the powerful coal barons, whose names once added luster to the industrial and political life of the State, went down in the crash, and their holdings passed into other hands. The new owners continued to operate the mines nonunion, and the hungry and defeated strikers slunk back to the pits.

Meanwhile, as Attorney General, I engaged the very able Prosecuting Attorney of Harrison County, the late Will E. Morris, to prosecute Jim Toney and the two culprits who blew up the mine in Barbour County. The three were convicted and sentenced to long terms in the penitentiary.

This northern uprising, however, was the last major conflict in West Virginia's coal fields. In 1933, under special Acts of Congress, the coal miners of the entire country were unionized and that ended all major "mine wars" and their accompanying bloodletting in the hills.

---

[3] Under the law, it was the duty of the Attorney General to represent the Superintendent of State Police in this proceeding. I assigned the case to W. Elliott Nefflen, Assistant Attorney General, but as it turned out there was nothing for him to do.

Part Six

THE DAWN OF A NEW ERA

Part Six tells of the union's three "bloodless strikes," of ghastly hunger that still stalks the hills, of rags and destitution, of a people who have lost hope. It also describes a few of the more recent dramatic incidents in these once coal-rich mountains.

Chapter 24

BLOODLESS STRIKES

Unionization of the coal miners in 1933, under Federal fiat, did not end strikes in the industry. It did, however, end all violence and bloodletting in such labor disputes—there were no nonunion miners to take the jobs of strikers.

Prior to 1933, a strike was confined to one mine or to a small group of mines in a limited area. This restricted the accompanying hardships to a few people, in a relatively small community. Neither the country as a whole nor its industries were in anywise affected. But with nation-wide unionization, a strike in the coal industry became a national calamity. Not only are the coal miners of the entire nation idle, but the jobs of millions of other workers are in jeopardy.

After national unionization and before signing the "Peace Treaty," referred to in the preceding chapter, John L. Lewis, president of the miners' union, called three nation-wide coal strikes. The first was while the Federal Government had control of all mines under the war-time powers of the President. Its purpose was to force Secretary of the Interior J. A. Krug, as Coal Mines Administrator, to accept Lewis' interpretation of the wage contract.

On November 18, 1946, the U. S. District Court in Washington enjoined Lewis and his union from calling a strike, and directed Lewis to order the miners to return to work, pending an interpretation of the contract by the courts. Both Lewis and his union refused to obey the order on the grounds that it violated the Norris-LaGuardia Act, which forbade injunctions against labor unions. But on December 4 this contention was overruled by Judge T. Allen Goldsborough, and they were both found guilty of contempt of court. Lewis was fined $10,000, personally, and his union $3,500,000; and the Court intimated that a continuing fine would be imposed for each day the miners remained out of the mines, so they scurried back to work.

Later, the Supreme Court upheld the judgment of the lower court, but reduced the union's fine to $700,000, which it paid.

Lewis and the operators failed to agree on a miners pension plan, and on March 12, 1948, he advised his union locals throughout the country that the operators had "dishonored their contract," and the response of the miners came with surprising swiftness. To them a "dishonored" contract meant "no contract," and the following Monday they refused to return to the pits, and a nation-wide coal strike was on.

As a first step in obtaining an injunction against the strike, under the Taft-Hartley Law, the President appointed a factfinding board to inquire into the "cause and circumstances" of the strike, and "whether the dispute is of such a character as to endanger the national health and safety," and directed the board to report as speedily as possible.

A court order forced Lewis to appear and testify before the board. Among other things, he said that he had not called a strike; that his letter of March 12 to his local unions was "merely an overdue report to the beneficiaries" on the present status of the pension fund; and that "in refusing to work the miners were acting as individuals."

The Board gave no credence to Lewis' story, and found that his letter of March 12 telling the miners that the operators had "dishonored" their contract was the actual cause of the strike; and that the strike was "of such a character as to endanger the national health and safety."

Immediately, the Federal Government obtained a temporary injunction against the strike from the U. S. District Court, ordering Lewis "forthwith to instruct all members of the United Mine Workers of America to cease the strike and immediately return to their employment." Lewis ignored the order, and was cited to appear in Court April 12 and show cause why he and his union should not be adjudged guilty of contempt of court; and at the same time to show why an injunction should not be issued against him and his union miners prohibiting a strike for eighty days, as provided by the Taft-Hartley Law.

In the meantime, on April 10, Lewis and the operators' committee agreed on the pension plan, and Lewis sent the following telegram to all local unions:

> Pensions granted. Agreement honored. Your voluntary cessation of work should be terminated.

Ninety minutes later, counsel laid these facts before the Court as Lewis' compliance with the "forthwith" injunction order to call off the strike. But the Court held that the telegrams were sent too late, and both Lewis and his union were adjudged guilty of both criminal and civil contempt of court. Lewis was fined $20,000, personally, and the union $1,400,000 on the criminal contempt conviction only. A year later, the Supreme Court affirmed the judgment of the lower Court, and both fines were paid by the union.

In the meantime, the Court also issued an injunction against Lewis and his union barring another strike over the pension dispute for eighty days, as provided by the Taft-Hartley Law.

To force the miners back to work, sentence on the civil contempt conviction was deferred ten days. Fearful of still heavier fines, and possibly a prison sentence, Lewis worked frantically during the interval to get them back on the job. At the resumption of the hearing, it appeared that practically all miners had returned to work, and sentence on the civil conviction was indefinitely postponed. Three weeks later the government dismissed the civil contempt charge against both Lewis and the union.

The losses to both miners and operators as a result of this strike were staggering. The welfare fund lost $4,500,000. The miners' loss in wages was $106,274,000, to which must be added the union's fine of $1,400,000, plus Lewis' fine of $20,000, which the union paid. In all, the miners had a total cash loss of $112,264,000; while the operators' loss in profits exceeded $150,000,000.

But the strike losses fell heaviest upon the general public. It lost 52,000,000 tons of coal. More than 200,000 workers in industries dependent upon coal were laid off for the last two weeks of the strike, and steel production dwindled to a mere trickle, at a time, too, when steel was the scarcest in years. *Iron Age*, a trade magazine devoted to the news of steel, said that approximately 1,500,000 tons of steel were lost by reason of this strike. "This loss," said the magazine, "is equal to the production of 300,000 automobiles, 20,000 farm tractors, 200,000 refrigerators, 200,000 stoves, 200,000 washing machines, 1,000 miles of 20-inch oil pipeline, 10,000 freight cars, and 14 oil tankers, all in very short supply at the time."

Without the operators realizing their true import, Lewis inserted in the 1948 agreement two innocent-looking provisions that gave him a life-or-death stranglehold on the entire coal industry. The first required the miners to work only when "willing and able," and the second empowered him to call them off the job at any time for "periods of mourning" for workers killed and injured in the mines during the year.

These provisions made the contract unilateral; that is, it bound the coal companies to keep their covenants, but left Lewis and his miners free and unimpeded. The miners could work, or not work, as it suited their whims; and Lewis could call them out at any time for indefinite "periods of mourning," without violating the terms of the agreement.

The operators maintained that Lewis used these two clauses to the great detriment of the coal industry, and demanded that they be eliminated from the next wage contract.

Lewis called two wage conferences, both to convene June 6, 1940: One at Bluefield for southern operators, and the other was at White Sulphur Springs for all other producers—the two points being about 40 miles apart. The conferees met sporadically for three and a half months. Lewis rarely appeared at either meeting and never announced his contract terms. During that time, however, Lewis called his miners from the pits on two occasions. One was a two-week mourning period, and the other for a week of "stabilizing inactivity." On September 19, he ordered a general strike throughout the country. But on November 9, he directed his miners to resume work for two weeks, and then to continue the strike.

By the middle of January, 1950, the Nation's economy was in dire straits. Its coal reserves were nearly exhausted; steel mills had laid off over 22,000 men; railroads had furloughed three-fourths of their freight crews; newspapers announced that 9,000,000 workers in coal-burning industries had joined the ranks of the unemployed; 372,000 coal miners were losing approximately $5,000,000 a day in wages; and the country's daily loss in coal production was 2,000,000 tons, normally mined each day.

The Nation faced economic disaster. But at last, a tardy Government in Washington decided to act. On January 19 the National Labor Relations Board filed a petition for an injunction before District Judge Richmond B. Keech to enjoin Lewis from making certain illegal demands upon the operators, and also, to force him to send his miners back to work on a 5-day work-week basis. A hearing was set for February 1.

On February 1, President Truman asked both sides to agree to a seventy-day truce, the miners to return to work on a 5-day work-week basis, and he to appoint a board to ascertain the facts, and recommend a solution. An answer was requested within forty-eight hours. The operators accepted immediately, but Lewis refused the President's request.

The Government immediately invoked all the provisions of the Taft-Hartley Law. On February 11, Judge Keech held the "willing and able" and "periods of mourning" clauses illegal, and enjoined Lewis from pressing for them. The Court also held that the "health and safety of the Nation" demanded the immediate resumption of coal production; ordered the miners back to work on a 5-day week basis; and directed Lewis and the operators to resume bargaining "in good faith" at once.

The next day Lewis ordered his miners to return to work, five days a week. They refused, and said: "No contract, no work." A second order by Lewis also was ignored, and again the miners answered: "No contract, no work."

The court-ordered wage conference got under way February 16, and four days later the miners' union was cited by Judge Keech for criminal contempt of court. Its trial began February 27 and ended March 2. In the meantime, the wage conference announced on Sunday evening, March 5, before the Court's decision on the contempt charge, that a wage agreement had been signed by the parties; and the next morning the destitute and hungry miners trooped back to the mines. Three days later the Court dismissed the contempt charge against the union.

In the new contract the "able and willing" clause was discarded; "periods of mourning" were limited to five days a year; wages were increased 70 cents a day, or to $14.75; the union shop was retained; tonnage payments into the welfare fund were increased from 20 cents to 30 cents a ton; and the contract period was for 28 months, or until July 1, 1952.

This strike lasted from September 19, 1949, until March 5, 1950, except for the 15 days Lewis permitted the miners to work in November. The workers lost 111 workdays by the strike, plus the 15 days lost by reason of Lewis' work-stoppages, or a total of 126 days. At $14.05 per day, the total heartbreaking loss of each miner was $1,770.30. At the time of the strike employed miners in the entire country numbered 372,000, and the group sustained a total cash loss in wages of $658,551,600; and their welfare fund lost over $50,000,000. In West Virginia the loss in wages of its 119,568 employed miners was the staggering sum of $211,630,360.

The miners gained a wage increase of 70 cents a day. Assuming that after the strike they had worked the full five days a week, it would have required ten years for that small increase to reimburse them for their actual monetary loss caused by the strike. "And the tragedy is," said a leading operator, "Lewis could have had these same terms on the first day of the wage conference on July 5, 1949, if he had not been too childishly stubborn to enter seriously into contract negotiations."

In view of the adverse rulings of the Court, the financial losses of the miners, and the ultimate destructive effects on the industry, the strike was a disastrous tragedy for the workers. "We called it the 'Great Strike,'" an unemployed miner told me, "not because we gained anything, but because we lost everything."

But the evening the contract was signed, Lewis gave a statement to the press that possibly boosted the miners' morale and made more palatable the losses they had suffered. "The United Mine Workers," said he, "have emerged from this struggle with additional bread and butter for their families, with additional life and death benefits for their ailing, with their union intact, with their membership unimpaired, and all labor benefitted by the discrediting of the Taft-Hartley abomination."

Just how the Taft-Hartley Act had been discredited, Lewis did not explain.

After hearing "General" Bill Blizzard, President of District 17 (Charleston) of the United Mine Workers, attack the Taft-Hartley Act as a "slave labor law," I asked him what was in the law that caused labor leaders to fear it.

"Oh, Hell," he said, "I don't know. I've never read it. The 'Old Man' (meaning Lewis) says to be against it. So, I'm against it."

"Do you suppose Lewis has ever read it?" I inquired.

"I doubt it," he replied. "He gets all that dope from the legal department. You know the 'Old Man' (meaning Lewis) always has to have a 'whipping boy,' and the Taft-Hartley Law makes a good one."

Chapter 25

DESPAIR AND HUNGER STALK THE HILLS

In 1933, when coal miners were unionized on a National scale, the country was in the depths of a depression. A few miners were working in scattered mines at starvation wages, and coal was selling at ridiculously low prices.

As the National economy improved, union leaders began their ceaseless struggle for a "reasonable wage" for miners. But, when wages reached the point of "reasonableness" these union leaders did not cease their demands for further increases. Each year, either by a strike or threat of a strike, they forced the coal companies to yield to their demands for higher wages and increased "fringe benefits," and coal prices had to keep pace with these wage increases.

After unionization, Lewis and a committee of operators would meet annually to work out a wage contract for the ensuing year. Always, Lewis was attended by a retinue of about one hundred economic advisers and the more intractable of his union leaders, while the operators' delegation was composed of about an equal number of their more rabid Lewis haters.

Usually, the conferees spent more time in wrangling and name-calling than they did in negotiations. In such an atmosphere, with rare exceptions, an agreement was impossible, and deadly strikes followed with staggering losses to the miners, operators, and the general public. In fact, so commonplace did these annual battles become that they came to be regarded by everybody as a *way of life*—one of the unavoidable incidents in the coal industry.

Shortly after the "Great Strike," the late Harry Moses, one of the Nation's more forward-looking coal men, appalled by the stupendous economic losses suffered by both operators and miners in these labor struggles, proposed that in the future both the union and operators abandon all violent, name-calling, mass-bargaining, wage conferences; that the operators designate one man to negotiate with Lewis alone; that those two work out all wage contracts without strikes or cessation of work; and that both sides agree in advance to accept such agreement when made. Both Lewis and the operators accepted the suggestions, and the latter named Moses as their sole bargaining agent. Why this idea was not advanced years earlier is a mystery—too simple, probably.

From that time until his untimely death from cancer, April 1, 1956, Moses and Lewis met annually and worked out new wage agreements, and both sides accepted them.

Moses was succeeded by Edward G. Fox, a coal man of Pottsville, Pennsylvania, who followed closely in the Moses tradition. Both Moses and Fox, however, were handicapped by the unyielding policy of Lewis, that the greater the concessions made by the operators in any annual wage contract, the larger and more unreasonable became his demands the following year. And, to avoid another disastrous strike and the further loss of markets, they submitted to his demands.

Late in September, 1956, Fox and Lewis had their first wage confrontation.[1] It was the same old story. A few operators said there were no negotiations; that Lewis simply handed Fox a previously-prepared contract, and, to avoid another strike, Fox signed it. This contract left the pension fund payments at 30 cents a ton; increased vacation time from 10 to 14 days; raised the "forced" vacation gifts from $140 to $180; and increased daily wages to $22.25 a day, a gain of $2.40.

But that was not the end. At each subsequent wage discussion, union leaders demanded and got an increase in wages and "fringe benefits." By the threat of a general strike, in the spring of 1964, union leaders forced the operators to approve a contract that boosted miners' daily wages to $28.25, raised "forced" vacation gifts to $225, but left pension payments at 40 cents a ton. And all this, too, when "portal to portal"[2] pay had reduced the average working day to six and one-half

[1] See Chapter 26.
[2] "Portal to Portal" means that the miner's day begins when he arrives at the mine entrance, and it ends when he arrives at the mine exit.

hours. Of course, this contract, like the others, resulted in higher prices for coal, loss of additional markets, more closed mines, more idle miners, and more families added to the relief rolls.

Fuel is the lifeblood of manufacturing, and during the Great Strike thousands of factories were forced to close their doors and furlough their employees. Many plants were idle as long as five weeks, and there was much distress among the workers.

Factory owners became alarmed at the prospect of having their plants closed every few months because of a miners' strike. They were concerned, too, about the rising coal prices, and the future promised no relief. Finally, to free themselves from the withering hand of an intransigent labor czar, who held a life-and-death stranglehold on their industries, they switched to either fuel oil or natural gas,[3] and this huge industrial market was lost to the coal producers.

In July, 1961, I said to a leading operator: "When you operators knew, as you must have known, that your concessions to the union's demands for higher wages and larger 'fringe benefits' eventually would force you to increase coal prices to a point that would destroy your markets, why didn't you call a halt?"

"That course was thoroughly considered by the operators," he replied. "There were two reasons why it was not followed; we knew that Lewis would call a strike, and we also knew that another prolonged work-stoppage would lose to us the few markets we had left; and we decided to hold our concessions to union demands as low as possible, mechanize our mines as rapidly as machines could be made, curtail the number of miners as fast as machines were installed; and thereby reduce mining costs to a point where we could compete with other fuels."

---

[3] The early 1950's saw the completion of the large natural gas pipe lines from Louisiana and the Southwest to the industrial East. And now much of the Atlantic seaboard is underlaid with a network of pipe lines that supplies this natural fuel to the general public.

The change from "pick-and-shovel" to machine mining is called "automation" or "technological advances" by the savants. But the more widely understood term is "mechanization," which means the substitution of powered machines for human muscle.[4]

In April, 1961, Bill Blizzard, head of District 17 of the miners' union (Charleston), announced to the newspapers that "mechanization of the State's coal mines was complete." What he should have said was that the "changes had been made in all mines where the owners intended to make them." He made no reference to hundreds of mine owners who for some reasons, financial or otherwise, had decided against making the switch, had closed their mines, and set their miners adrift—to be added to the relief rolls.

Of course, the purpose of this change in mining methods was to reduce the number of miners, and thereby lower the cost of producing coal. And so effective was the change that on January 1, 1962, the number of unemployed miners in the State constituted a major economic disaster. In 1950 the State's employed miners numbered 119,568, but as of January 1, 1962, that number had dropped to 31,734, a reduction of 87,734, or 73 per cent of the State's mining force. Allowing a wife and two children to each miner (a modest estimate), on that date approximately 300,000 people in the State had been added to the relief rolls.

However, not all of the displaced miners remained in the coal fields. When machines stole their jobs, those workers who still had youth, ambition, the capacity to learn other trades, and the ability to adapt themselves to a new environment, took their families and migrated to large industrial

---

[4] These powerful machines, called "continuous miners," are too technical to be described here. They are made in different sizes for use in coal seams ranging from 28 inches to nine feet. The one I saw had a large revolving cylinder studded with huge teeth at the front. It would tear into a coal face with an upward turn that swept the coal backward onto a conveyor belt on the machine. This belt carried the coal to the rear of the machine and dumped it onto another belt that started it on its way to the surface. The instructor who was explaining the machine said that one of the larger machines would mine more coal in 24 hours of continuous operation than 100 pick-and-shovel miners would mine in 30 days.

centers. Thus, in the decade between 1950 and 1960, the coal counties lost one third of their population; and people are still leaving the areas.

Many of the displaced workers who still live in the coal fields are too old to be accepted in other industries. Others lack the ambition and initiative to change to new and strange surroundings. Still others lack the mental capacity to learn new skills. But whatever the reasons, a very large number of former miners and their families still remain in the coal counties and pose a serious economic problem.

Chapter 26

SUNDOWN IN THE HILLS

On October 3, 1956, Lewis presented to the National Convention of the Union in Cincinnati his first wage agreement "negotiated" with Edward G. Fox a few days before. In asking for its ratification by the Convention, he said: ". . . it is the best contract ever obtained by the miners,.... It encompasses all that the industry can stand at this time. There isn't any more. If there was, you would have gotten it."

The next day an operator said to me that it would have been more in keeping with the facts if Lewis had said to the Convention: "We have bled the patient until he is white and very weak. Any further bleeding at this time is certain to cause his death. We will let the patient recuperate somewhat, and then we shall bleed him again next year."

The evening of the day this contract was approved by the Convention, I stopped for gas on the outskirts of a mining village in southern West Virginia. A group of unemployed miners sat and stood around the gas station. Presently, they were joined by another unemployed worker, who came from the village, a half-mile below. He carried an evening newspaper that told of the approval of the contract by the Convention; and as he joined the group, he jubilantly exclaimed: "Look, boys! 'Old John L.' sure has brought home the cream this time."

We listened while one of the group read the news story. When he had finished, a young miner remarked: "Well, 'Old John L.[1] may have brought home some cream, but he sure as hell has let the cow go dry."

"What do you mean?" I asked.

"Look around you," he answered. "Here are nine men, all

---

[1] The beetle-browed, bushy-haired, craggy-faced, unsmiling John Llewellyn Lewis, who headed the coal miners' union and fought their battles for forty years, died Wednesday night, June 11, 1969, in a Washington, D. C., hospital, age 89 years.

unemployed. Some of us have not worked for months. Five are idle because machines are now doing the work they once performed. Four were employed in a mine that is now closed—not because the coal is exhausted, but because of the high cost of mining. It can no longer be operated at a profit. There are hundreds of these closed mines in the State and thousands of miners in the same fix we are in."

"What do you think changed these once prosperous communities into areas of economic desolation?" I asked the young man.

"Oh! I don't know," he answered. "May I ride down to the town with you?"

In the car he said: "In this union one has to be careful what one says, and where he says it. Are you connected with either the operators or the union?"

I assured him that I had no connection with either group, and he continued: "I do have some very decided opinions as to what brought about these changed conditions in the coal fields."

I stopped the car at the village and said: "Wait a minute. You don't look like a miner, and you certainly don't talk like one. First, tell me something about yourself."

"Possibly I have had more advantages than most miners," he replied, "but I am a miner. I am a high school graduate, and I have had three years in college. But I got married and had to go to work. I worked in the mines one year after I finished high school, then did my stint in the army. I also worked in the mines during summer vacations between college years, and I have been in the mines since leaving college. I am 28 years old."

"Now," I said, "I am anxious to hear how a very intelligent young miner views the present situation in these coal fields."

"The present plight of the miners and many operators," he began, "is due to a combination of three things: the ever increasing cost of mining coal, the steady increase in the use of mining machines, and the switch of heretofore large users of coal to other fuels.

"The disagreement is over the cause of these changes. But one does not have to be an economist to know that mining machines are installed to reduce the labor costs of mining the coal; that the switch to other fuels is due to the high price of coal, the uncertainty of the supply, and because the same results can be obtained from the cheaper fuels; and that the exorbitant price of coal is due largely to the excessively high wages paid the miners, and the so-called 'fringe benefits' the operators have been forced to pay the workers.

"Apparently, it has been the aim of our union leaders to get a higher and higher daily wage written into each successive annual contract, regardless of the ultimate effect on the industry. These leaders have failed to understand that every unreasonable advance in wages and 'fringe benefits' simply meant more mining machines, closing more mines, and permanently idling more miners.

"Take this contract we just read. Lewis described it as the 'best contract in the history of the industry.' But it cannot help the miners who have already lost their jobs, and it will do much harm to many who are now working. It will further increase the cost of mining coal, cause more machines to be installed, close more mines, and add more thousands to the ranks of the unemployed.

"This situation has no end. Next year, and the next, and the next, the union leaders, with the approval of the working miners, will be back clamoring for, and they will get, other wage increases with the same results. It is a situation where the 'blind lead the blind,' and the end is foretold in Holy Writ—'both shall fall into the ditch'."

"What do you intend to do now?" I inquired.

"I am through with the mines," he said. "While I am out, I am going to stay out. My wife has her college degree, and I have arranged to return to college next semester and graduate. Then we shall enter upon a new life, possibly teaching."

"That is fine for you," I said, "but what about those eight unemployed men we left back at the gas station, the thousands of others who are now like them, and the still other thousands soon to be added to their ranks? What can they do?"

"They will have to go elsewhere," he said.

"Yes, but where?" I asked.

He hesitated, then slowly shook his head, and said: "They can't remain here. Economically, these coal fields are dying. In a few years nothing will be heard in large sections of these mountains except the hoot of the owl and the eerie cry of the whippoorwill. But, in time, these ugly mining scars, that now mar the landscapes, will disappear from the mountainsides and this whole region will become beautiful National and State forests."

Then, suddenly glancing toward the West, he exclaimed: "It is sundown! I must go home!" and he was gone.

As I drove down the valley, again and again I said to myself: "How true! It is SUNDOWN in these hills."

Chapter 27

EPILOGUE

During my 1961 summer tour of these mountain coal fields, I noticed that the large operations were working, at least part time, while most of the smaller plants were closed, and their facilities falling into decay. I asked a number of former small operators why they gave up the coal business. Always, the answer was the same: "Loss of coal markets, high cost of mechanizing mines, and the 'take-it-all' policy of the union leaders." A few said: "I just grew tired of working for the union, with no rewards for myself."

I ended my 1961[1] tour by attending a Sunday evening church service in an almost deserted mining camp. The camp had been closed for months, but many of the unemployed workers still lived in the tumble-down shacks. The miner-preacher was leaving the community, and this was his last message to his bewildered flock. It was a moving scene, and one that could have been enacted that night in hundreds of the State's coal camps.

The text was from Hosea, Chapter 8, verse 7: "For they have sown to the wind, and they shall reap the whirlwind." From it that uneducated coal miner and mountain preacher developed a sermon that our better educated and more sophisticated city ministers could never equal. It had in it that "something plus" which came from more than thirty years working and living in the coal fields.

Later in the evening, with some corrections in English, I recorded in my notebook my recollection of the preacher's closing remarks, as follows:

"Brethren, I have been digging coal and preaching the Gospel in these coal fields for more than thirty years. During

---

[1] In the summer of 1967, 1 again toured these same coal fields and found conditions even worse than they were six years earlier—hunger, rags, misery. Intervening years and kindly death, however, had removed many of the more aged from the relief rolls.

that time I have experienced much and seen more. I have seen men working at reasonably good wages and their wives and children happy. I have seen dozens of strikes, four in one year, mines closed, men idle, women and children ragged and hungry. I have seen men assaulted, beaten, yes, even murdered by their fellow workingmen, when their only crime was that they needed to work, wanted to work, and tried to work. I have seen miners and mine owners, who should have been allies and friends, tearing fiercely at each other's throats, until now both are destroyed. Both sides have sown to the winds of avarice and greed; and both sides are now reaping the whirlwinds of bankruptcy, hunger, misery, and despair.

"Through the years I have lived among you, I have tried to bring peace, relieve distress, soothe the aching heart, cool the fevered brow, comfort the bereaved. I regret that I could not do more.

"From my long association with these people I have learned that the three predominating emotions of coal miners and their wives are despair, frustration, and hope: despair over the past, frustration over the present, and hope for the future. But now I see no future in these mountains, and all hope is gone. I love these mountains, I was born here, I have spent my life here, my friends are here, my wife is buried here. But now, jobless and penniless, I must take leave of my native mountains and the friends of a lifetime and begin a new life with my son in a distant city. I am loathe to go, but no other course is open to me.

"Over and over again I have asked myself, just as you have asked yourselves: 'Why? WHY? Why are men idle in these coal fields with all the work there is to do? Why are their wives and children hungry and in rags?' Brethren, we must face the facts. There is but one answer. Our leaders, both union and industrial, have failed us. They have lacked the vision necessary to bring about cooperation between mine owners and their workers. And it is recorded in Holy Writ: 'Where there is no vision, the people perish.'

"But now, I must bid you, and each of you, an affectionate farewell."

Then stretching his long, gaunt arms out toward and over his congregation, he thus blessed them:

"And now may the Lord bless you and keep you: May the Lord make His face to shine upon you, and be gracious unto you. May the Lord lift up his countenance upon you and give you—PEACE.*

With eyes moist with tears, that congregation of beaten men and broken women rose and went slowly, silently, out into the night.

*Numbers, Chapter 6, verses 24, 25, and 26.

Appendixes

Appendix I

NOTES

All committee reports and supporting evidence cited in these pages, and West Virginia newspapers of the strike periods, are on file in the Department of Archives and History, Capitol Building, Charleston, West Virginia.

Note I

Chapter 2—BLACKLIST: Almost from the beginning of the industry coal companies maintained a kind of clearing house through which they furnished each other with the names of discharged workers, and the reasons for their discharge. Frequently, the names of such persons were put on a "blacklist" and thereafter they were industrial outcasts—unable to get a job in the fields.

Note 2

Chapter 2—CRIBBING: From the beginning coal was brought from the interior of the mines in small cars designed to hold a specified weight of coal. But the companies "cribbed" their miners by building a "crib" or frame around the top of these cars until they held from 500 to 1,000 pounds more coal than the workers were paid for mining. For a judicial discussion of this system of labor larceny, see the case of *Rhodes vs. Coal Company*, Vol. 104 West Virginia Supreme Court Reports, page 450, where a miner recovered $3,000 for mining "cribbed" coal. But that was one case among many thousands of similar instances where suits were never brought.

Note 2-a

PART TWO-THE U. S. SENATE BORAH COMMITTEE:

This committee, headed by Senator William E. Borah, of Idaho, was directed by the Senate to investigate conditions in the strike areas of Cabin Creek and Paint Creek, in West Virginia. The committee sat for days in the city of Charleston, and heard testimony from coal operators, union leaders, strikers, mine guards, bankers, and local businessmen. Printed copies of all evidence taken and the committee's report to the Senate are on file in the State's Department of Archives and History, in Charleston. This evidence and committee report supplied much of the source materials for Part Two of this book.

Note 3

Chapter 2—DOCKING: In cases where a company's check-weighman at the tipple decided that a miner had left too much slate and rock in his car of coal, he "docked" such miner by arbitrarily reducing his total mined coal tonnage as much as the weighman's whim dictated. The miner had no remedy. I have heard miners say that the waste in their car, if any, did not exceed ten pounds. Yet, they were "docked" from 500 to 1,000 pounds. Operators have told me that it was their policy "to dock miners considerably more than the waste in their cars." This was done, they said, "to punish the miner and make him more careful in the future, and warn other miners that they had better send clean coal to the tipple." But whatever the purpose, it was still labor larceny.

Note 4

Chapter 2—THE DONAHUE AND SENATOR BORAH COMMITTEES: In the fall of 1912 Governor William E. Glasscock appointed Bishop P. J. Donahue, of the Catholic Church, Hon. Fred O. Blue, State Tax Commissioner, and Capt. S. L. Walker, of the State Militia, as a committee to ascertain the cause of the Cabin Creek and Paint Creek strike. Also in the Spring of 1913, the U. S. Senate appointed a Committee, headed by Senator William E. Borah, of Idaho, to investigate the same strike.

My discussion of this strike in Part Two is based upon the

findings of the above named committees, Reports of the State's Department of Mines for the years 1912 and 1913, judgments of the military courts, decisions of the State Supreme Court, Charleston newspapers of the strike period, conversations with the former strike leaders, and my personal observations and experiences in and near the strike zone.

Note 5

Chapter 3—MOTHER JONES: Aside from what is stated in her ghost-written autobiography, published in 1920, little is known of the early history of Mother (Mary) Jones. In it she says that she was born in Ireland in 1830, came to America in 1835, taught school in Michigan and Tennessee, married and widowed in 1867, became a dressmaker in Chicago, and then a union organizer. From that time until age made further activity impossible she was in the forefront inciting violence in every major labor disturbance in America. She died in Maryland, near Washington, in 1931, at the age of 100 years.

Note 6

Sections 4 and 12 of Article III of West Virginia's Constitution, referred to in Chapter 6, read as follows:

Section 4: The privilege of the writ of habeas corpus shall not be suspended. No person shall be held to answer for treason, felony, or other crime not cognizable by a justice, unless on a presentment or indictment of a grand jury.

Section 12: The military shall be subordinate to the civil power, and no citizen, unless in the military service of the State, shall be tried or punished by any military court, for any offense that is cognizable by the civil courts of the State.

Note 7

Chapter 3—BALDWIN-FELTS DETECTIVE AGENCY: This was a labor-baiting, strikebreaking organization owned and operated by William G. Baldwin and Thomas L. Felts, with its home office in Bluefield, West Virginia. From 1909 to 1925 my law office was on the third floor and this Agency occupied the entire fourth floor of the same building. During that time I became intimately acquainted with both Baldwin and Felts, and knew scores of their employees, including the seven killed at the Matewan Massacre.

But this detective agency was a great civilizing influence in the southern mountains. The Norfolk and Western Railroad follows Tug River. In some places it is in Kentucky; at other points, West Virginia. When the road was first constructed in the late 1880's and 1890's, many mountaineers in both states made a practice of breaking into freight cars containing interstate shipments of goods and taking what they wanted. After the Baldwin-Felts men had killed a few such thieves and sent a number to prison, the practice ended. These detectives also rendered valuable aid to local law enforcement officers in the arrest and prosecution of criminals in no way connected with the coal industry.

Note 8

Chapter 8—AUTHOR'S NOTE: As a spectator, I attended the last three days of the first Matewan Massacre trial, listened to the closing arguments of counsel, and secured the group photograph of the defendants and the foreman of the jury that acquitted them.

STATEMENT BY JUDGE ROBERT D. BAILEY: As Circuit Judge of Mingo County, I presided at both Matewan Massacre trials. I have read Chapters 7 and 8 of Mr. Lee's book, and they accurately tell the story of the killings as it was related at the trial by the State's witnesses. The trial incidents mentioned, actually occurred.

Signed: R. D. Bailey

Pineville, W. Va.
June 28, 1961.

Judge Bailey died in October, following my visit with him in his office on June 27, 1961.

H.B.L.

Note 9

Chapter 9—AUTHOR'S NOTE: I knew "Buster" (George) Pence, notorious Baldwin-Felts mine guard, for several years before and after the killing of Sid Hatfield and Ed Chambers. Many times, I heard him make the remark, "Kill 'em with one gun, and hand 'em another one," when he would be boasting of his cleverness in some of the bloody incidents in his career as mine guard and strikebreaker.

His stratagem simply meant that he put a recently fired pistol in the dead hand of his victim, and then claimed that the deceased shot at him first, and he fired only in self-defense.

Note 10

PART FOUR—GOVERNOR CORNWELL'S COMMITTEE: In 1919, Governor John J. Cornwell appointed Colonel George S. Wallace and Major Tom B. Davis as a committee to investigate conditions in the Logan County coal fields. They held protracted hearings in the town of Logan.

U. S. SENATE KENYON COMMITTEE: In 1921, the United States Senate appointed a committee, headed by Senator Kenyon, of Iowa, to investigate conditions in all of West Virginia's coal-producing areas. This committee also conducted hearings in Logan.

Each committee heard testimony from coal operators, strikers, mine guards, union leaders, public officials, and local businessmen; and each committee filed its report with the proper officials.

The source materials of Part Four of the book were the testimony taken by those two committees, news items in contemporary newspapers, the voluminous records of court proceedings, and my personal experiences in Logan County.

Note 11

Statement of Hon. Vincent Legg:

As his Executive Assistant, I was familiar with the official acts of the late William G. Conley during his term as Governor of West Virginia, 1929-1933. I have carefully read Chapters 17, 18, and 19 of Mr. Lee's book, and they accurately relate the official actions of the Governor with respect to Logan County, at the time and in the matters described in said Chapters.

(Signed) Vincent Legg

Charleston, W. Va.
June 29, 1961.

Statement of Frank Gibson:

I have read Chapters 17, 18, and 19 of Mr. Lee's book, and insofar as they relate to my presence and participation in the events described in such Chapters, they are true.

(Signed) Frank Gibson

Princeton, W. Va.
June 27, 1961.

Note 12

Statement by Judge R. D. Bailey:

I was employed by relatives and friends of Roy Knotts to assist the Attorney General in the prosecution of his murderer, Enoch Scaggs. I was present at every phase of the trial, actively participated therein, and observed every incident in connection therewith. I have read Chapter 18 of Mr. Lee's book, and every statement made therein concerning the trial is true.

(Signed) R. D. Bailey

Pineville, W. Va.
June 28, 1961.

Note 13

PART FIVE—U. S. SENATE GOODING COMMITTEE: In 1928, the United States Senate appointed a committee, headed by Senator Frank Gooding, of Idaho, to investigate conditions in the coal fields of Ohio, Pennsylvania, and West Virginia. The committee, however, devoted its entire time to the strike areas in northern West Virginia. It took 3,414 pages of testimony (two large volumes) from coal operators, strikers, mine guards, public officials, and local businessmen.

The main source materials for Part Five of the book were the testimony taken by the committee, reports of the State Police, newspapers of the period, the many court proceedings growing out of the strike, and my personal visits to and observations and experiences in the strike area.

Note 14

STATEMENT OF HON. SAM. T. MALLISON: I was Governor Howard M. Gore's Executive Assistant during his term as Governor of West Virginia, 1925-1929. Prior to that time I lived in the city of Clarksburg, West Virginia, in the heart of the State's northern coal fields. I have read Chapters 20 to 23, inclusive, of Mr. Lee's book, and they accurately portray conditions in those fields of which I had personal knowledge; and, according to my recollection, also correctly state the facts respecting the Governor's official acts concerning the prolonged strike described in said Chapters.

(Signed) Sam T. Mallison

Pittsburgh, Pa.
July 31, 1961.

ISOLATED INCIDENTS OF UNION TERRORISM

ASSAULT ON CLIFTONVILLE

After being closed two months because of a strike, the Richland Coal Company, at Cliftonville, in Brooke County, in the northern field, resumed operations in July, 1922, on a nonunion basis. A dozen guards were employed to protect the property against attacks by union miners employed just across the State line in Pennsylvania.

On Saturday evening two weeks later, the superintendent of a Pennsylvania mine five miles away telephoned Cliftonville that the union miners were mobilizing for the expected attack. Sheriff Duvall of Brooke County and five of his deputies joined the mine guards to assist in repelling the invasion.

During the night four hundred armed miners, many of them foreigners and unable to speak the English language, assembled on the hills overlooking the mine. At daybreak the mongrel mob surged down upon the camp from three sides, its leaders shouting: "Come on boys, let's git the goddamned scabs."

The attackers fired the first shot from an improvised cannon made from a 4-inch steel pipe loaded with powder and small pieces of scrap iron. It was aimed at the company store, but the charge went wild and struck the roof of a dwelling, without serious damage. The firing then became general and lasted about thirty minutes. The guards fought from the protection of buildings and had one man slightly wounded, while the attackers were forced to fight in the open and had six killed and a number wounded.

After setting fire to the mine headhouse, the attackers retreated, hotly pursued by the guards who wounded a number and captured fifteen prisoners. Sheriff Duvall became separated from the other officers and failed to return. An hour later a searching party found his bullet-riddled body in the nearby woods. His pistols were gone, but a few feet from his body three of the attackers lay dead.

One Slovak prisoner, who spoke only broken English, was asked by Governor E. F. Morgan, who visited the jail, why he came from Pennsylvania into West Virginia to kill working—men like himself. With a shrug of his shoulders, he replied: "This free country—me kill anybody me no like."

Burning headhouse and conveyor at Cliftonville.

A special grand jury was convened in Brooke County, which returned indictments against 250 attacking union miners. Four were tried, convicted, and sentenced to ten years in the penitentiary. Seven confessed and received sentences of from four to eight years, including an officer of the Cliftonville local union. Thirty others, including the presidents of the Donahue and Cedar Grove local unions, both in Pennsylvania, pleaded guilty and were sentenced to three years each. All remaining indictments were dismissed.[1]

---

[1] These facts were given to me at the time by the then Prosecuting Attorney of Brooke County.

DESTRUCTION OF WILLIS BRANCH

In 1919, the refusal of Willis Branch Coal Company, in Fayette County, to contract with the miners' union precipitated a local labor war that lasted eighteen months, brought death to a number of persons, and completely destroyed the mining camp—with a property loss of more than a half million dollars.

Motivated largely by jealousy, in the political campaign immediately preceding this strike, the late William McKell, himself a very large operator, and a number of other Republicans revolted against what they called the "boss rule" of Sam Dixon, head of the Republican party in the county, and the county's largest coal producer. They also protested against the political influence of the "Fayette County Whiskey Ring," in which they said Dixon was interested.

This so-called Whiskey Ring was a corrupt gang of politicians, liquor dealers, saloonkeepers, and bribe givers, that ruled the county. No one could obtain a saloon license in the county unless he was approved by it, and every saloonkeeper in the county was compelled to purchase his stock from a wholesale liquor house in Charleston owned by members of the "Ring."

Failing to wrest control of the Republican organization from Dixon, the dissidents joined with the Democrats and elected Henry McGraw, a retired coal miner, as sheriff. Later, when the strike developed, the Sheriff sided with the strikers and refused to give any protection to McKell's Willis Branch operation, whereupon the strikers enjoyed a "Roman Holiday"—pillaging, destroying, and killing. McKell said: "This is my punishment for having supported the goddamned union son-of-a-bitch."

This attitude of the Sheriff compelled the coal company to employ the Baldwin-Felts mine guards to protect its property and nonunion workers. But the location of the camp, in a deep valley between high hills, and the long haul from the mine south to the tipple, made an adequate defense impossible.

Early in the struggle the strikers broke into the local express office and stole a machine gun and several thousand rounds of ammunition consigned to the mine guards, which they repeatedly used with disastrous effect on the camp. A year and a half later, "Old Peg Leg" Lawrence Dwyer, a union organizer, turned this same machine gun over to the marching miners, and it was used by them in the "Battle of Blair Mountain."[2]

Several times the company attempted to operate the mine, but every attempt brought a fusillade from the hills. Finally, after the tipple, power house, and railroad trestles had been destroyed, the camp was abandoned. Fire, dynamite, and bullets had reduced the village to a shambles and rendered it uninhabitable.

A few local union leaders were sent to the penitentiary for these crimes. But Jim Toney, the most notorious of the outlaws, escaped detection. In 1924 Toney moved his base of criminal operations to Fairmont, in the northern coal fields, where he was sentenced to the penitentiary for a number of years for attempting to blow up the Monongah mine, in Marion County.[3]

During the strike, the union sent a national representative to Willis Branch to urge the strikers to continue the fight. This connected the national organization directly with the destruction of the company property.

The coal company brought suit in the Federal Court against the union and its leaders for one million dollars damages for the wilful destruction of its property. The national union officials settled the case before trial; but apparently they did not want the rank and file of its members to know how much of their money had been used to pay for the lawless acts of a few criminals, and they exacted a promise from the company officials and their attorneys not to divulge the amount paid.

In 1950, however, the late Judge W. L. Lee (not related to

[2] See Chapter 13.
[3] See Chapter 22.

me), of Fayetteville, one of the attorneys for the coal company, said to me: "You will be safe in saying that the union paid in excess of $100,000 in currency, as a compromise settlement of the case." But, in the fall of 1962, the late Charles E. Mahan, prominent Fayetteville lawyer, and one of the attorneys for the coal company, told me that the amount actually paid was $400,000.

THE SHOOTING UP OF GLEN WHITE CAMP

E. E. White was the owner of the Glen White coal operation in Raleigh County. In the fall of 1917, the union undertook to organize his miners, and about one-third of his 200 workers joined.

Immediately, the dissidents demanded recognition of their new union and the "closed shop." White refused their demands and a strike was called at the plant. The nonunion miners, however, ignored the call and continued working.

A month later, Old Mother Jones suddenly appeared on the scene. At a mass meeting of the strikers she made one of her characteristic incendiary speeches, in which she said:

> "You goddamned cowards are losing this strike because you haven't got the guts to go out and fight and win it. Why in the hell don't you take your high-power rifles and blow the goddamned scabs out of the mine."[4]

A few days later, Tony Stafford, an unnaturalized Italian and a union organizer, procured a number of rifles and cached them in the woods on the mountainside overlooking the mine. This was a shaft operation, and the workers were lowered into the mine and brought to the surface by means of an elevator-cage that would carry about fifty men.

In the afternoon of November 16, 1917, Stafford, Tony Sorazzo, also an unnaturalized Italian and president of the

---

[4] Mr. White had a reporter take this speech. It was used later in an injunction suit against the union.

new union, and seven other strikers assembled at the point where the guns were hidden. When the loaded elevator came up, they began firing at the men in the cage. The operator of the hoist quickly lowered the cage back into the mine, and no one was injured. The officers later picked up more than 300 empty rifle shells in the area.

Evidence at the later trials disclosed that the rifles were furnished by "Old Peg Leg" Lawrence Dwyer,[5] a member of the Executive Board of the United Mine Workers of America (the miners' union), who lived in the town of Beckley. Embittered by the loss of a leg in a mine accident, he hated all coal operators, and had become a fearless old "rabble-rouser" for the union. It was further said at the time that the basement of his house was a storage place for rifles and ammunition kept for use in the union's labor wars. A few months after the Glen White shooting, Old Peg Leg's house burned, and city firemen were afraid to approach the burning structure. As the fire raged, frequent explosions were heard; and after the fire died out, the old man would not permit a search of the ruins.

After the shooting the culprits scattered, and it took nearly a year for the detectives to round them up. Some were found in the coal mines of Wyoming, others in Kentucky, and a few in Pennsylvania. Stafford and Sorazzo were jailed in Raleigh County. The other seven were brought to the office of the agency in Bluefield, where they all signed written confessions.

The nine strikers were indicted in Raleigh County for attempted murder. Stafford was convicted and sentenced to the penitentiary for five years, and his conviction and sentence were approved by the Supreme Court.[6]

Because of local prejudice against defendants all remaining cases were transferred from Raleigh to Pocahontas County,

[5] This was the same Lawrence Dwyer who delivered the machine gun stolen by strikers at Willis Branch to the marching miners in the Armed March. See Destruction of Willis Branch, preceding item, and also Chapter 13.
[6] For a full discussion of this bizarre case, see *State vs. Stafford*, Vol. 89 West Virginia Supreme Court Reports, page 301, etc.

where Sorazzo was convicted and sentenced to five years in the penitentiary. Upon completion of their sentences both Italians were deported by the Immigration Authorities. Two defendants testified for the prosecution and they were dismissed. The other five confessed in open court and were sentenced to three years each in the penitentiary.[7]

THE RAPE OF WIDEN

The Widen mining camp nestled among the hills in a remote section of Clay County, fifty miles northeast of Charleston, employed about 250 miners, and produced over one-half million tons of high quality coal annually.

When the miners were unionized nationally in 1933, the Widen miners refused to join the United Mine Workers, and organized their own union. The company encouraged this action, and paid its miners from two to four dollars per day more than the union scale. This greatly irked the union overlords, and they began a systematic and prolonged campaign to smash the "company union," as they called it, and force the workers to join the national organization. That this would reduce the daily wages of these miners to a level of the union scale was of no concern to those "dedicated labor patriots."

At the insistence of the labor "bosses," the (U. S.) Labor Relations Board would call an election among the Widen miners every two years to determine which of the two unions should represent them as their "bargaining agent." That they lost every election made no difference to the union leaders. A month before an election they would call in "goon squads" from Kentucky and Pennsylvania to reinforce a contingent of strongarm West Virginia thugs; and these combined gangs of hoodlums would then move in on the little village of Widen.

---

[7] I was subpoenaed as a standby witness in both of these trials. At the request of Tom Felts, as a notary public, I had sworn each of the defendants to his written confession. If the defendants, or any one of them, had repudiated his confession I would have been called as a witness. None did, and I was not used.

Their object was to beat up, threaten, intimidate, and coerce the miners into voting against the company union, and to destroy company property, paralyze transportation, stagnate production, and to commit other crimes, even murder, in an all-out effort to force the company to stop supporting the local union.

These armed gangs encamped on the hills overlooking the village. A dozen or more automobiles filled with thugs were constantly parked along the only road entering the town, and nothing was allowed to pass without their inspection and approval. Two railroad trestles on the only railroad serving the community were blown up and burned three or four times. They planted a bomb in the car of the mine superintendent, and when he touched the starter he and the car were blown to bits. A father was shot and killed when he went to the aid of a crippled son who was being beaten by the terrorists. And citizens of Clay County advise me that not one of these criminals was ever punished for his crimes.

These murderous assaults on Widen were due solely to the late Bill Blizzard, president of District 17, United Mine Workers union, with headquarters in Charleston—the same Bill Blizzard who led the miners' Armed March in 1921, and who was later tried for treason and murder. He imported the goon squads, frequently visited their camp, and made numerous speeches to the mob.

During one of these biennial Widen battles I drove from Charleston to the village to see what was really taking place. Eight or ten cars were parked beside the road, and probably twenty men were either sitting in cars or milling about nearby. Two armed men stopped me, but when I told them I was a friend of Blizzard they welcomed me. I parked on the roadside and listened to Blizzard as he harangued the mob. "We have to get rougher and tougher with these goddamned scabs," he shouted. "We must win this election." But he lost every election.

Two years later, while another battle was in progress at Widen, I talked with Blizzard in a Charleston hotel lobby.

"How is your Widen campaign coming along?" I asked.

"Good," he answered. "I think we are going to win this time."

"The papers say that your boys are playing it rough up there. How about it?" I queried.

"0, Hell! We are just doing peaceful picketing," he replied. "It's the other crowd that is dishing out the rough stuff."

"You know, Lee," he continued, "Widen is my baby. I am paying all the expenses up there myself. If we don't win this time, I'll try again, and I'll keep on trying until I bring that damned 'Big Mogul'[8] up there to his knees." And in Blizzard's obituary in the *Charleston Daily Mail*, August 1, 1958, in referring to the Widen outrages, it is stated that at a "labor clinic (whatever that is) to which he had been invited as a speaker, Blizzard declared the strike was his... that he was financing and directing the ill-fated miners strike."[9]

These biennial Widen battles continued through the years, with the same results, until March, 1955, when Blizzard was dismissed as the head of District 17 of the United Mine Workers Union. In 1957 the Widen mine was sold and the new owners invited the United Mine Workers Union to come in, and the company union ceased to exist. A few months later, however, the mine was closed and its 250 workers and their families were added to the relief rolls.

---

[8] By "Big Mogul," Blizzard referred to Colonel J. G. Bradley, principal owner and general manager of the Widen mine when these outrages took place.
[9] These statements were not true. Blizzard did not have the money to finance such undertakings, and these "dedicated labor bosses" are careful not to spend their own money in such ventures. The statements were made for the purpose of protecting the union, should it be sued by the coal company.

KEYSTONE AND THURMOND

Every mushroom town in West Virginia's early coal fields felt the impact of the imported criminal element from Europe and our Southern States. But the most notorious of such towns were Keystone in McDowell County and Thurmond in Fayette County. They are discussed separately.

KEYSTONE

Keystone!

This Sodom and Gomorrah of McDowell County's early coal fields is on the Norfolk and Western Railroad, fourteen miles east of the town of Welch. It lies along both sides of polluted Elkhorn Creek, which joins Tug River at Welch. The Tug, in turn, flows into the Big Sandy River.

When I went to Bluefield in June, 1909, the pastime of the morbidly curious was to "slum Keystone's Cinder Bottom." It was," they said, "a revelation of human depravity."

Indeed, what was said of "Thurmond on the C.&O." also applied to Keystone—"The only difference between Keystone and Hell is Keystone has a small stream of black polluted water running through it."

It was two years, however, before I had an opportunity to visit Keystone. In June, 1911, I accompanied a client to the town of Northfork to aid in closing a real estate deal. We finished our work by mid-forenoon and since there was no return train until late in the afternoon, we decided to walk the mile and a half down the track to Keystone. At the City Hall we slipped a five-dollar bill to the Chief of Police and asked him to guide us through "Cinder Bottom." The Chief thought "it was a little early, as the ladies might not be up yet," and told us to return at one o'clock.

As we walked up the street, the Chief observed: "To see this 'Barbary Coast' at its best or worst, whichever way you look at it, you should come between nine and twelve o'clock at night. They sure do whoop it up then."

"Chief, what is the population of the town?" I asked.

"About 2,500," he replied, "and Negro and foreign-born miners make up at least seventy-five percent of that number. Of course, there are many fine people here—mine superintendents, merchants, doctors, dentists, store clerks, school teachers, and their families, but they are a small minority, and most of them are afraid to leave their homes after dark. They are here because they have to be here—not from choice. There are also a number of honest Negroes and European immigrants here, trying to make an honest living. The remainder of the population, however, is made up of white and Negro saloonkeepers, bartenders, roustabouts, gamblers, bouncers, thieves, prostitutes, pimps, white slavers, and panderers."

At the upper end of the town was a small bottom covered two feet deep with cinders from nearby coke ovens. On this strip of land, called "Cinder Bottom," were about 25 old, dilapidated houses. Curtains at the windows, however, indicated that they were occupied. Waving his hand toward them, the Chief said:

"Well, here it is—the infamous 'Cinder Bottom,' known far and wide as the 'International Whorehouse District of the Coal Fields'—the toughest of the country's tough spots. In addition to America's white and Negro prostitutes, their likes are here from nearly every country in Europe. That gives the place an international flavor. In these dives all barriers are down, and there is complete racial, social, and sexual integration."

In the first house we entered we were met by a short, fat, stringy-haired, coarse-featured, Hungarian Madam who shrieked at the Chief: "What the hell you do back? Me paid you off yisteday." The Chief gave her a clout beside the head that sent her reeling against the wall, and said: "You damned old bat, you speak only when I speak to you." Later the Chief explained that he had "collected her rent yesterday."

We were taken through eight houses. They were wholly integrated—racially, socially, and sexually. From eight to ten girls in each house, bossed by a tough-looking old Madam. The Chief said there were about the same number in each of the other houses, except there were a few more in a couple of "all-colored houses" at the upper end of the Bottom. Each house had a large room with benches around the walls and a player piano in a corner. These rooms were used for drinking and dancing when the denizens were "Whooping it up" at night.

In one house we saw a white girl on the lap of a Negro man, both drinking beer from the same bottle. In another house a Negro girl and a white man were swigging beer from a common bottle. The Chief opened a few bedroom doors as we passed through the houses. In one bed we saw a white man and a Negro girl. In another house, it was the reverse—a Negro man and a white girl in the same bed. In some houses we saw girls moving around, some in nightgowns, others in panties and bras, and in one house we saw two girls clad only in smiles.

As we returned to the City Hall, I said to the Chief:

"Chief, at the first house, you mentioned collecting the rent. Who owns these dives?"

"That is a matter that is never discussed," he replied.

"Chief," I continued, "how is your crime rate in the town, high or low?"

"Very high," he replied. "And it runs the gamut of crimes—theft, rape, robbery, murder. Never a week passes without at least one murder. Some weeks as many as three or four. As you came down from Northfork you no doubt noticed that deep railroad cut through the spur of the mountain, just above town. We call it 'Dead Man's Cut.' All too frequently a man is robbed and murdered and his body dumped into it to be ground up under the wheels of the numerous passing coal trains."

"Chief, how did all this criminality fasten itself on McDowell County?" I next asked.

"In the first place," said he, "this coal field is new, and in a very isolated region. To attract and hold miners our operators pay the highest wages paid in any coal field in the country. Therefore, these thousands of miners furnish fruitful pickings for the thugs, thieves, gamblers, and prostitutes who always flock to those places where money flows freely and law enforcement is lax."

"Chief, it is about train time, but one more question.

"It is apparent that the coal operators control the county and its officials. Why don't they tell these local officers to clean up this filth that seems to pervade the whole county?"

"I have heard the operators' explanation of this many times," he said. "It is their contention that the entire economy of the county, and the value and permanency of their huge investments are wholly dependent upon the brawn of the thousands of colored and foreign-born miners employed in the county; and that these workers would not remain in the county without the 'gaiety, entertainment, and accommodations' that go with the ready presence of 'wine, women, and song.' Therefore, they demand a wide-open county, and the local authorities cooperate fully."

It was 50 years later, June, 1961, before I again visited Keystone. The town had fallen upon evil days and was just another "ghost town" of the coal fields. Only one mine was working, and it only part time. At least three out of every five business places in the town were vacant, and their entrances clogged with piles of dirt, paper and other rubbish blown in by the wind. Small groups of unshaven, poorly clad, and beaten men lingered and talked in some of the doorways. Here and there small clusters of unkempt, ragged, hungry-looking children played hopscotch on the sidewalks.

My brother, Russell Lee, who accompanied me on the tour quietly said: "Look up at the windows." I raised my eyes cautiously. Mountain folk sometimes are resentful of what they consider "intrusive attention." At a number of second- and third-story windows sat aged-looking women, with wrinkled faces and gnarled hands, their elbows cushioned on pillows placed on window sills, and their chins cradled in their cupped hands. Some stared fixedly toward the mountaintops, while others looked stoically down upon the almost deserted streets—pictures of utter frustration and hopelessness.

We talked with the youthful, educated, and enthusiastic Mayor of the town. He had prepared himself for the legal profession and had been admitted to the bar, but because of economic conditions was still assisting in his father's furniture store. "The picture looks dismal," he said, "but I am hopeful of an upturn in the coal industry soon. In fact, it is bound to come. Of course, it will never be like the old days, but things will get better." He could have added: "They can't get worse."

The Mayor was too young to know much about the infamous "Cinder Bottom" of former years. But, in answer to my inquiry, he said, apologetically: "There are still a few girls up there."

Apparently, a vacant storeroom across the street from the Mayor's store was being used by some religious organization. Hanging inside the front window was a large streamer-like sign, done in red letters a foot high, that would have been an appropriate admonition for the Keystone of an earlier day. It read: GIVE GOD A CHANCE

At the town of Welch, a few miles down the Elkhorn gulch from Keystone, I talked with an "old-timer" in the McDowell County coal fields.

"Tell me about Keystone," I said.

"Well, there ain't much to tell," he replied. "It is just another one of the hundreds of coal field ghost towns—men unemployed, and women and children ragged and hungry. Only one mine is working at Keystone, and it only part time. The miners, the money, and the 'Cinder Bottom Floozies' are gone, and most of the people who are still there are living on 'handouts' from the State and Federal governments. Even the

town's past iniquities are forgotten by everybody—EXCEPT
GOD."

THURMOND

While serving as Director of the State's Department
of Archives and History, Honorable Kyle McCormick
did a good deal of research work into the early history
of the notorious mining town of Thurmond on New
River in Fayette County. In 1959 he published his
findings along with a picture of famous Dunglen
Hotel, in his very splendid book, The New-Kanawha
River and the Mine War of West Virginia. With Mr.
McCormick's permission, I reproduce here his story
of Thurmond and picture of the Hotel.

It is doubtful whether any of the boom cities of the West
could surpass the story of Thurmond, West Virginia, in the
matter of wild colorful history all taking place in the early
part of the twentieth century. The town is on the New River
and at the junction of the Loop Creek branch and the main
line of the Chesapeake and Ohio Railway in Fayette County.

It is the only town in the East located in a canyon. It was
named for Captain W. D. Thurmond of the Partisan Rangers
of the Confederate Army. Thurmond was built by Thomas
G. McKell, who through his wife inherited 12,500 acres of
coal lands in Fayette County from her father, John Dunn. Mr.
McKell built a ten-mile branch of railway to his coal lands and
gave it to the Chesapeake and Ohio Railway. That was in the
nineties.

Mr. McKell built the famous Dunglen Hotel in 1901 at
Thurmond and it was then that life in Thurmond really
picked up. This was a hundred room, three story structure

---

[1] In the summer of 1968 I again saw Keystone. The seven intervening
years since my last visit had brought no change in the appearance of the
town—except for the worse. A relief worker in Welch, however, said that
during those years death had removed permanently about thirty of the
more elderly unemployed from the public relief rolls. "In time," she said,
"death solves all problems."

with wide veranda, and all the latest conveniences and frills. Alden Pence Butterfield came from Cincinnati to operate the hotel, and with him came a Cincinnati orchestra for an opening dance at which 100 couples enjoyed the evening. Included in this list were some of the more prominent names of West Virginia.

Then for the next thirteen years in the Dunglen Hotel, the bar never closed, nor did the gambling room nor the poker game. It was only when West Virginia went dry in 1914 that the bar closed. In addition, five other saloons opened up in Thurmond. It was said that one could get about anything he wanted at the Dunglen or any other place in town.

The famous (or infamous) Dunglen Hotel.

The coal operators, newly rich and dripping with profits, threw their big parties at the Dunglen, which were second to none. The hotel was filled every night with traveling men, business men, coal operators, gamblers, adventurers, harlots, and every type of person.

There was a slogan on the Chesapeake and Ohio at that time: "No Sunday west of Clifton Forge and no God west of Hinton."

Harrison Ash, a Kentuckian, was police officer of the town, and he was another Wild Bill Hickok—a terror to evil doers. [He was six feet four inches tall and weighed 275 pounds.]

The poker game is said to have lasted 14 years, the longest poker game in history. Dead men were no novelty in the river or elsewhere in town. A dead man was found in the river with $80, a watch, a pistol—he was fined the money and the watch for carrying a weapon and buried in the local Potter's field. Ash's pistol had seven notches [filed] upon it.

Local conventions were held and the meetings called to order by pounding the rostrum with a Colt .45.

However, business was good in Thurmond. In a town of 500, there were two banks, five saloons, the 100-room Dunglen [Hotel], and a local newspaper. The town originated more freight for the railway than any place on the line including the city of Cincinnati.

Among the amusements were cock fights, and at one time a fight between dogs and a wildcat. Through Thurmond came special cars bearing theatrical troops to perform at a magnificent opera house at Glen Jean, five miles away, another McKell town.

There might be as much as $50,000 on the table at one time in a Dunglen poker game.

But prohibition cooled off the town a bit, and good roads and a bad name finished it. One bank failed, the other moved to Oak Hill.

Rev. Shirley Donnelly of Oak Hill, a noted historian, wrote of Thurmond: "The only difference between Hell and Thurmond was in that a river ran through Thurmond."

In 1930, the Dunglen Hotel burned down and that ended the wild life of the town.

Today, Thurmond is just another station on the Chesapeake and Ohio, with only one passenger train in either direction making it a stop.

Its glory, if such it may be called, has gone.

Captain H. W. Doolittle was a poet and conductor on the Chesapeake and Ohio and wrote of Thurmond in its heyday:

You have heard of the California gold rush,
Way back in forty-nine
But Thurmond on the New River
Will beat it every time.
There's people here from everywhere,
The colored and the white;
Some mother's son bites the dust
Almost every night.
On paydays, they come to Thurmond
With a goodly roll of bills,
Some gamblers get their dough,
And they sneak back to the hills.

Some, though ne'er return alas!
And they meet a thug—
We find them on the railroad track
Or in the Thurmond jug.
Where handy is the blackjack
And the price of life is low
At Thurmond on New River,
Along the C. and O.,
Where men are often missing
After the drinker's fight,
And the crime laid onto the river
And the trains that pass at night.

AUTHOR'S NOTE: A few weeks before my graduation at Marshall College (now Marshall University), in June, 1905, the college president, Dr. L. J. Corbly, told me that he had recommended me for the principalship of the Thurmond school, and suggested that I visit the town before accepting or declining the position.

I arrived at the town and the Dunglen Hotel about five o'clock on a Friday evening. After supper as I sat in the hotel lobby watching the milling crowd, in walked a giant of a man. He wore a gaudy uniform, with the word "CHIEF" on his broadbrimmed Stetson hat. He took a chair near me. I went over to him, introduced myself, and told him why I was there. His name, he said, was Harrison Ash, the town's only policeman.

Chief Ash told me much about the town's lawlessness, took me to see the hotel's famous poker game, and, in parting, said: "Son, you are a likely-looking young man, trying to get a start in the world, and my advice to you is, stay away from this hell-hole."

I returned to Huntington the next morning without even contacting the school authorities.

INDEX

Agents, labor, 4, 5
Allen, Walter, 111
Anderson George, 148
Anderson, J. A., 53, 55
Anderson, J. R., 53
Armed March, Chapter 13, beginning at page 94
Atwood, Nat, 61

Bailey, Judge Robert D., 62, 129, 190, 192
Baldwin-Felts mine guards, 11
Baltimore Agreement, 144
Bandholtz, General H. H., 98, 101
Barbour County mine explosion, 153
Barrackville mine explosion, 153, 155
Belcher, Attorney A. M., 104
Bennett, Oscar, 53, 55
Bethlehem Steel Company, 144, 145
Bishop Donahue Committee, 18, 19, 20, 22, 188
Bittner, Van A., 119, 144, 147
Blacklist, 11, 18, 19, 187
Blair Mountain, Battle of, 100, 101
Blankenship, Sheriff, 52
Blizzard, Bill, 16, 25, 98, 105, 106, 110, 112, 171, 175, 201, 202
Blizzard, Gordon, 93
Blue, Fred O., member Donahue Committee, 188
Blue Goose, 116
Boorher, A. J., 53, 56
Borah Senate Committee, 16, 35, 36, 187,188
Borah, Senator Wm. E., 16, 82
Bowman, Bill, 61
Bradley, Col. J. G. (Widen), 202 (footnote)
Brockus, Capt. J. R., 98
Browning, Lon, 122
Buchanan, R. C., 53, 55
"Bull Moose" special train, Chapter 5, beginning at page 38
"Bull Pen," The, (military jail at Pratt), 33
Burgraph, Fred, 61

Cabell, Charley, 24, 45
Cabin Creek and Paint Creek, location of, 15
Cabin Creek and Paint Creek strike, (all of Part Two), pages 95 to 147, inclusive
Cafalgo, A. C., 100
Calvin, Lee, 39
Chafin, Don, pages 87 to 121, inclusive
Chambers, Judge C. C. (footnote), 130
Chambers, Ed, pages 63 to 70, inclusive
Chambers, Hallie, 61
Chambers, Reece, 61, 63
Charles Town, Jefferson County, 107
Cincinnati (miners') Convention, 177
Clay, Van, 61
Cliftonville, attack on, 194, 195
Coal, exploitation of, 4
Coleman, Bowser, 61
Conley, Governor Wm. G., 122, 124, 125, 134
Consolidation Coal Company, 144
Cornwell, Governor J. J., 91; Committee, 94, 191
Coverlee, Rev. Robert, 132
Cribbing, 18, 19, 187
Cunningham, C. B., 53, 55, 56
Cunningham, Dan, 93

Damron, Judge James, 51
Davis, Major Tom B., 74, 75
Docking, 18, 188
Donahue, Bishop, Committee, 18, 19, 20, 22, 188
Dunglen Hotel, 209
Dwyer, Lawrence ("Old Peg Leg"), 97, 199

Educated miner speaks, 178
Elliott, Adjutant General, 16, 20
England, E. T., Attorney General, 89, 90
Everettville mine explosion, 153
Explosives stolen by strikers, 151, 159

Farmington mine explosion, 153
Fayette County, site of last Armed
    March trials, 114
Federal troops in Logan County, 101
Federal troops in Mingo County, 74,
    77
Felts, Albert, 20, 53, 56, 60
Felts, Lee, 20, 53, 56, 60
Felts, Thomas L., 11, 53,66
Ferguson, J. W., 53, 55, 56
Ford, Capt. George M., 43
Fox, Edward G., 173
Francis, James D., 136, 137

Gas, natural, lines to the East, 174
Gaujot (Go-show), Tony, 21
Gibson, Lieut. Frank (Red), pages 125
    to 138, inclusive, 192
Glasscock, Governor Wm. E., 26, 31,
    33,34
Glen White mine shot up, 198, 199,
    200
Goldsborough, Judge T. Allen, 165
Gooding Senate Committee, 144, 146,
    148, 193
Gore, Governor Howard M., 111, 151,
    152, 153
Gore, John A., 100
Gould, Valley, 116
Greenbrier County, Bill Blizzard's trial
    in, 112
Greggs, Floyd, 99

Harrah,G.C., 113,114
Hatfield, Anse, 59
Hatfield, Sheriff Bill, 67
Hatfield, Cap, 117
Hatfield, Governor Henry D., 43, 44,
    46
Hatfield, Sheriff Joe, 122, 129, 130,
    134, 135, 138
Hatfield, Sid, pages 52 to 70, inclusive
Hatfield, Tennis, 116, 117, 119, 120
Hatfield vs. Scaggs, 90 (footnote)
Hays, Arthur Garfield, 116
Heiser, J. L. (Tobe), 91
Herndon, Judge I. C., 70
Hickey, G. C., 113, 114

Higgins, C. T., 53, 55, 56
Hill, Sheriff Boner, 38, 39, 40
Hill, Dr. J. O., 132, 133
Hill, Dr. Wade F., 60, (footnote) 61,
    62
Hitchman Coal & Coke Company, 79,
    80
Holt, Savoy, 113
Hoover, President, 81
Houston, Harold, Attorney, 106, 107,
    114
Howard, Judge B. F., 51
Huntington bricklayer, murder of, 99
Huntington, Rev. Henry L., 116

Iron Age, magazine, 168

Jackson, Judge Naaman, 122, 123,
    124, 125, 126, 130, 133
Jones, James Elwood, 82
Jones, Old Mother (Mary), 26, 33,
    40, 44, 96, 97, 189
Joyce, Attorney Claude A., 130
Jurors from Monroe County, 125,
    127, 128, 130, 131

Keech, Judge Richmond B., 169
Keeney, Frank, 25, 96, 97, 98, 104,
    105, 106, 111, 114, 115
Kenyon, Senator, Senate Committee,
    92,191
Kermit, village of, 51
Keystone, town of, 203
Kisser, C. H., 61
Knotts, Roy, murder of, 123, 125
Krug, J. A., Fuel Administrator, 165
Kump, Governor Herman Guy, 139

Labor Agents, 4, 5
Lavender, A. D., habeas corpus, 77
Lawson, Dr. S. B., 132
Lazelle, Judge I. Grant,148
Lee, Howard B., 8 (footnote), 10, 27
    (footnote), 29 (footnote), 40, 43,
    44, 45 (footnote), 46, 51 (footnote),
    52 (footnote), 63, 70, 71, 72, 93,
    96, 106, 110, 114, 122 to 140, 151,
    152, 153, 161, 171, 174,

177 to 183, inclusive, 211
(footnote)
Legg, Vincent, 192
Lewis, John L., 115, 147, 165 to
173, inclusive, 177, 178, 180
Lively, Everett, 60, 62, 67, 68, 70, 145
Logan City Council, 122
Logan County, location of, 85, 87
Logan Courthouse, 87
Losses due to strikes, 167, 169
Lucas, Hughey, 68, 70 (footnote), 101

McCarr mining camp, 73
McClintic, Judge George W., 117, 118
(footnote)
McGraw, Sheriff Henry, Fayette
County, 196
McKell, William, 196, 197, 198

Mahan, Attorney Charles E., 198
Mallison, Sam T., 193
Martial Law in Mingo County, 74,
75, 77
Martial Law on Cabin and Paint
Creeks, 30, 32, 39, 40
"Matewan Massacre," 52 to 57,
inclusive
Matewan, village of, 52 to 57, inclusive
Mayor Testerman, killed, 55
Mayor Testerman's wife married Sid
Hatfield, 57
Merimac mining camp, 73
Miliken, Dr., 101
Military Court on Cabin and Paint
Creeks, 33, 35
Miller, J. R., murdered Ed Reynolds
and J. W. Swanner, 113
Miner preacher, A, 181, 182, 183
Mining Machines, 175
Mingo County, Location of, 49
"Mingo Militia," 75
Mohawk mine shot up, 65
Monongah mine explosion, 155
Mooney, Fred, 104, 105
Morgan, Governor E. F., 74
Morris, Floyd E., 51 (footnote)
Morris, Will E., Attorney, 161
Morton, Quinn, 38, 39
Moses, Harry, 172

Mountaineer, A, speaks in court, 109
Mounts, Ben, 61
Mullins, Robert, 55
Muncy, George, 100, 112
Murray, Philip, 101, 102

Nance, S. F., 36, 37, 41 (footnote)
New River coal field, 80
Norris, Senator George W.
(Nebraska), 82

O'Connor, Col. Robert E., 151, 152
Operators in Politics, 8, 9
Osenton, Attorney C. W., 104, 108

Paint Creek and Cabin Creek,
location of, 15
Parker, Judge John J., 81,82
Pence 'Buster" (George), 67, 70,
145, 191
Petry, Bill, 92
Phaup, W. W., 27
Phonograph, hymns, used in trial, 112
Politics, operators in, 8, 9
Powell, E. O., 53, 55
Pratt, village of, site of "Bull Pen," 33

Red Jacket Coal Company, 52, 78
"Red Necks," 99, 106
Reynolds, Ed, murdered witness, 113
Rhodes vs. Coal Company, judgment
for mining cribbed coal, 187
Robinson, Judge Ira E., and martial
law, 42

Salter, Bill, 53, 54, 67, 68, 70
Scaggs, Emmett, 119, 131
Scaggs, Enoch, murderer of Roy
Knotts, 123 to 133, inclusive
Slot machines, 122
"Smilin' Sid"—moving picture, 58
Sorazzo, Tony, 198
Stafford, Tony, 198
Stanfield, Clomar, 99
Stringer, Robert, killed on Cabin
Creek, 27
Sullivan, Jess, 140
Supreme Court sustains martial law, 41
Swanner, J. W., murdered witness, 113

Taylor, Speaker J. Alf and Don Chafin, 119

Testerman, Mayor, killed at Matewan, 55

Testerman's widow married Sid Hatfield, 57

Tetlow, Percy, 115

Thurmond, Walter R., 133 (footnote)

Thurmond, Town of, 208 to 211, inclusive

Tinsley, Tot, killed at Matewan, 55

Toiler, Lee, 61

Toney, Jim, 161, 197

Townsend, Tom C., miners' attorney, 105, 106, 108

Tug, The Three Days Battle of, 73

Van Fleet, C. J., miners' attorney, 67

Walker, Capt. S. L., of Donahue Committee, 188

Wallace, Col. George S., Chairman Cornwell Committee, 95, 191

Watson, Clarence W., of Consolidation Coal Company, 143,144

Whiskey Ring, Fayette County, 196

White, Freeland, 133

White, H. S. (Sol), 55, 59 (footnotes)

White, Mastin, 116

White, Oscar, 133

Wilburn, Rev. J. W. and son, 110, 111

Wilkinson, Jack, denounces Chafin, 119

Williams, Art, 61

Williamson, Town of, 51

Willis Branch, destruction of, 196, 197, 198

Woods, Judge John Marshall, 108

Yellow-Dog Labor Contract, 78 to 83, inclusive